D1703877

Ferdi Kräling
Helmut Zwickl

michael schumacher

Schumi

Faszination
einer Karriere

KRÄLING FOPA

Impressum

(c) BY FERDI KRÄLING

59955 Winterberg
Tel.:   02983-97280
Fax: 02983-972828

IDEE, KONZEPTION UND REDAKTION
Ferdi Kräling Motorsport-Bild-Verlag

VERLAG UND VERTRIEB
HEEL Verlag GmbH
Wintermühlenhof
53639 Königswinter
Tel.:   +49-2223-92300
Fax: +49-2223-923026

TEXT
Helmut Zwickl

TEXTBEARBEITUNG
Kaye + Wilfried Müller (Engl.)
Alberto Noceti (Ital.)

FOTOS
Bodo und Ferdi Kräling

ARTWORK / DESIGN
Werbstatt
Thomas M. Simon
59955 Winterberg-Siedlinghausen

TITELGESTALTUNG
Thomas M. Simon

LITHOGRAPHIE
Tschimben Litho

DRUCK
Druck- u. Verlagshaus
Erfurt GmbH

PAPIER
nopa Coat Gloss (TCF)
170 g/qm doppelt gestrichen
Bilderdruckpapiere der
Nordland Papier AG, Dörpen

Printed in Germany

ISBN 3-89365-628-6

BILDNACHWEIS
Fotos: Bodo und Ferdi Kräling

außerdem :
Agentur Focus / Stefan Warter 6   *   ASA / Wolfgang Groth 4   *   ATP / Thill 1   *   Auto Bild: Ulrich Sonntag 1   *   Autosport: Jason Woods 1   *   Stefan Binder 1   *
* Reproduktion, sowie Text-und Bildauszüge sind nicht gestattet. Die Verwertung der Texte und Bilder, auch auszugsweise, ist ohne Zustimmung des Verlags urheberrech

Inhalt

4 Vorwort Niki Lauda
6-11 Ferrari - Einstieg
12-15 Jugendzeit
16-17 Kart 1984-1987
18-21 1988 Formel König / Formel Ford
22-29 1989-1990 Formel 3
30-31 Zuhause
32-33 Jürgen Dilk / Fan Club
34-43 1990-1991 Gruppe C / Mercedes
44-49 1991 Formel 1 - Jordan
50-73 Formel 1 - Benetton Der Weg zum ersten Formel 1 - Titel
74-75 Willy Weber - der Manager
76-77 Schumi - Fans
78-83 Fitness und Freizeitspass
84-99 Formel 1 - Benetton 2. WM-Titel
100-125 Das erste Jahr bei Ferrari
126-127 Familie
128-143 Das zweite Jahr bei Ferrari
144-147 Statistik
148-151 Schumi II

rgen Dilk 17 * Stefan Eder 3 * Reporter Images 4 * Daniel Reinhard 1 * Rainer Schlegelmilch 1 * Ulrich Upietz 4 * Weber-Management / Paul Schinhofen 1
d strafbar. Dies gilt auch für Verfielfältigungen, Übersetzungen, Mikroverfilmungen und für die Verarbeitung mit elektronischen Systemen.

NIKI LAUDA

Michael Schumacher wurde zu einem Elementar-Ereignis. Sein Aufstieg, seine Erfolge, seine Weltmeistertitel, sein Gang zu Ferrari erzeugten Emotionen, das Automobil-Land Deutschland zog sich daran hoch, Autofahren war wieder IN, so wie Tennisspielen IN war als Boris Becker von Sieg zu Sieg eilte.

Michael bringt jene entscheidenden fünf bis sechs Zehntelsekunden in ein Team ein, die die Konstrukteure meistens nicht mehr finden. Das ist der Schumacher-Faktor.

Eine außergewöhnliche Karriere verlangt nach einem außergewöhnlichen Buch, hier wird es von zwei Formel 1 – Profis vorgelegt. Ferdi Kräling hat die großen Momente fotografisch eingerahmt, Helmut Zwickl hat sie mit Fußnoten versehen.

Und dem Michael wünsch' ich, daß er mit Ferrari Weltmeister wird.

Niki Lauda

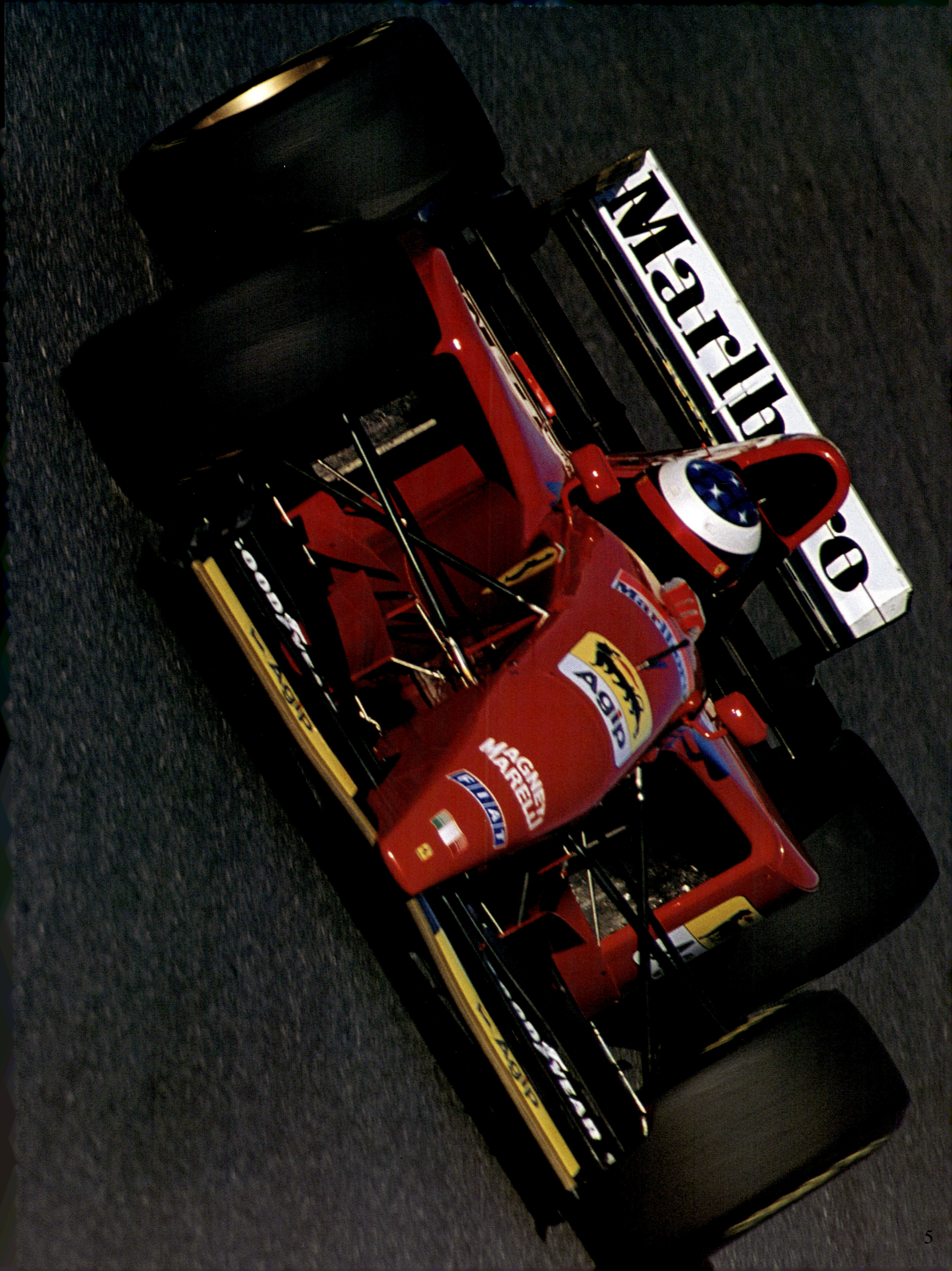
Agip
MAGNETI MARELLI
FIAT

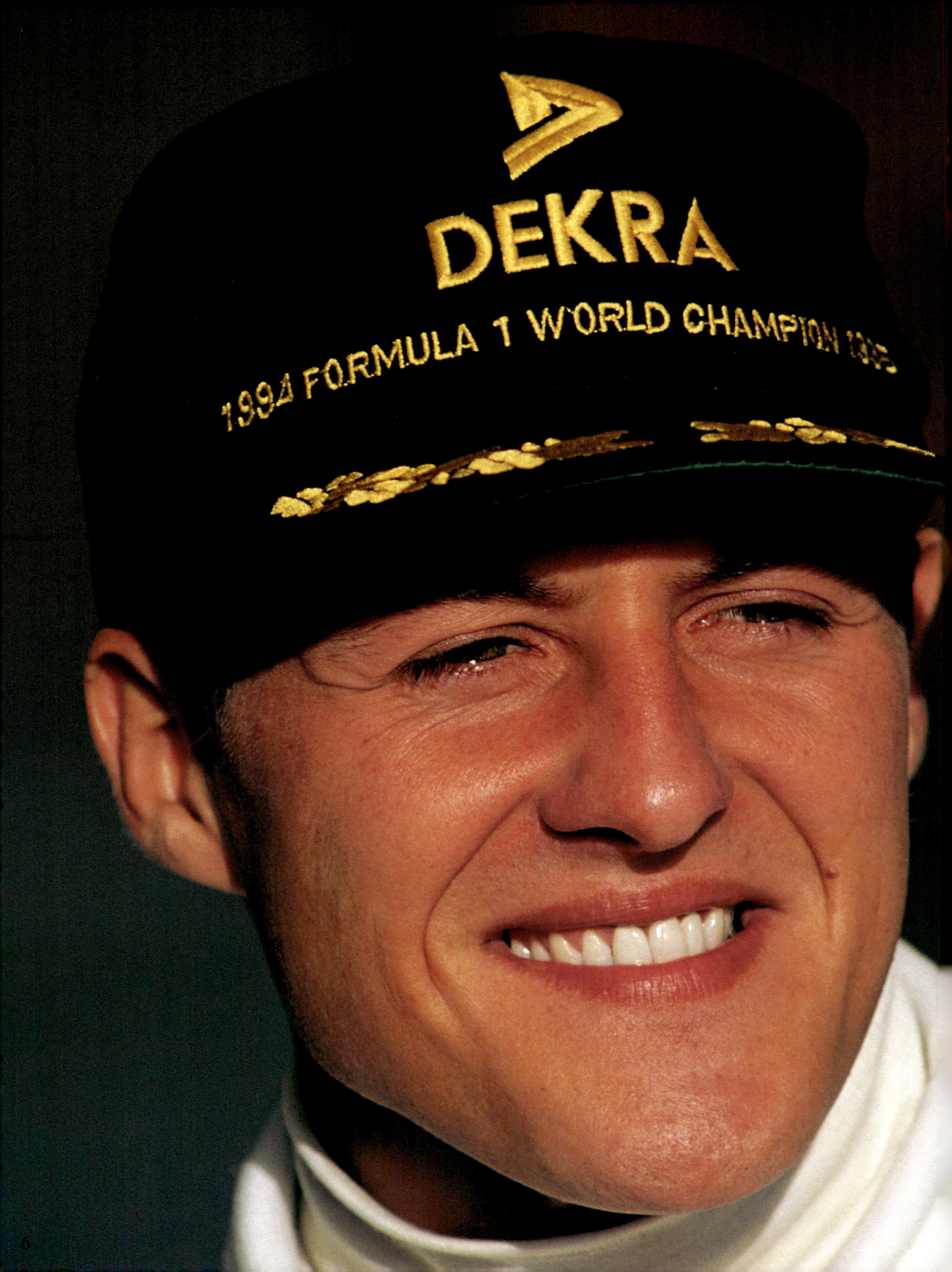
DEKRA
1994 FORMULA 1 WORLD CHAMPION

Es ist die Begabung. Ludwig van Beethoven wäre vermutlich nie ins Ferrari-Team gekommen und Michael Schumacher kann keine Symphonien komponieren, Albert Einstein hätte im Berg-Kraxeln gegen Reinhold Messner den kürzeren gezogen. Was Michael Schumacher von Natur aus auf sein Genplättchen mitbekam, tritt in dieser spezifischen Vollendung äußerst selten auf.

It's a gift. Ludwig van Beethoven could very probably never have joined the Ferrari Team, and Michael Schumacher could certainly not compose a symphony. Albert Einstein had no chance in climbing mountains against Reinhold Messner, and what Michael Schumacher received in his genes from nature is found very rarely in such specific perfection.

Questione di doti innate: Ludwig van Beethoven molto probabilmente non sarebbe mai arrivato alla Ferrari, Michael Schumacher non sa comporre una sinfonia, e come scalatore Albert Einstein avrebbe senz'altro perso il confronto con Reinhold Messner... le doti iscritte nei cromosomi di Michael Schumacher non si esprimono spesso con questa perfezione.

Countdown to launching off towards the boundaries of physics...

Countdown zum Abschuß an die Grenzen der Physik...

onto alla rovescia per la partenza verso i limiti della fisica...

Sein Erfolg mobilisiert die Medien, die Medien bestimmen seinen Wert, sein Wert bestimmt sein Einkommen, wer Schumi nicht im Cockpit hat, muß gegen ihn wettrüsten. Und das kommt noch viel teurer...

His success mobilises the media, the media determine his worth, his worth decides his income, and those who don't have Schumi in the cockpit must be in the arms race against him. And that is much more expensive...

Il suo successo mobilita i media, i media determinano il suo valore, il suo valore determina il suo reddito. Chi non ha Schumi al volante deve "armarsi" a dovere. Il che viene a costare ancor di più...

michael schumacher

EIN PORTRÄT

A PORTRAIT

UN RITRATTO

13

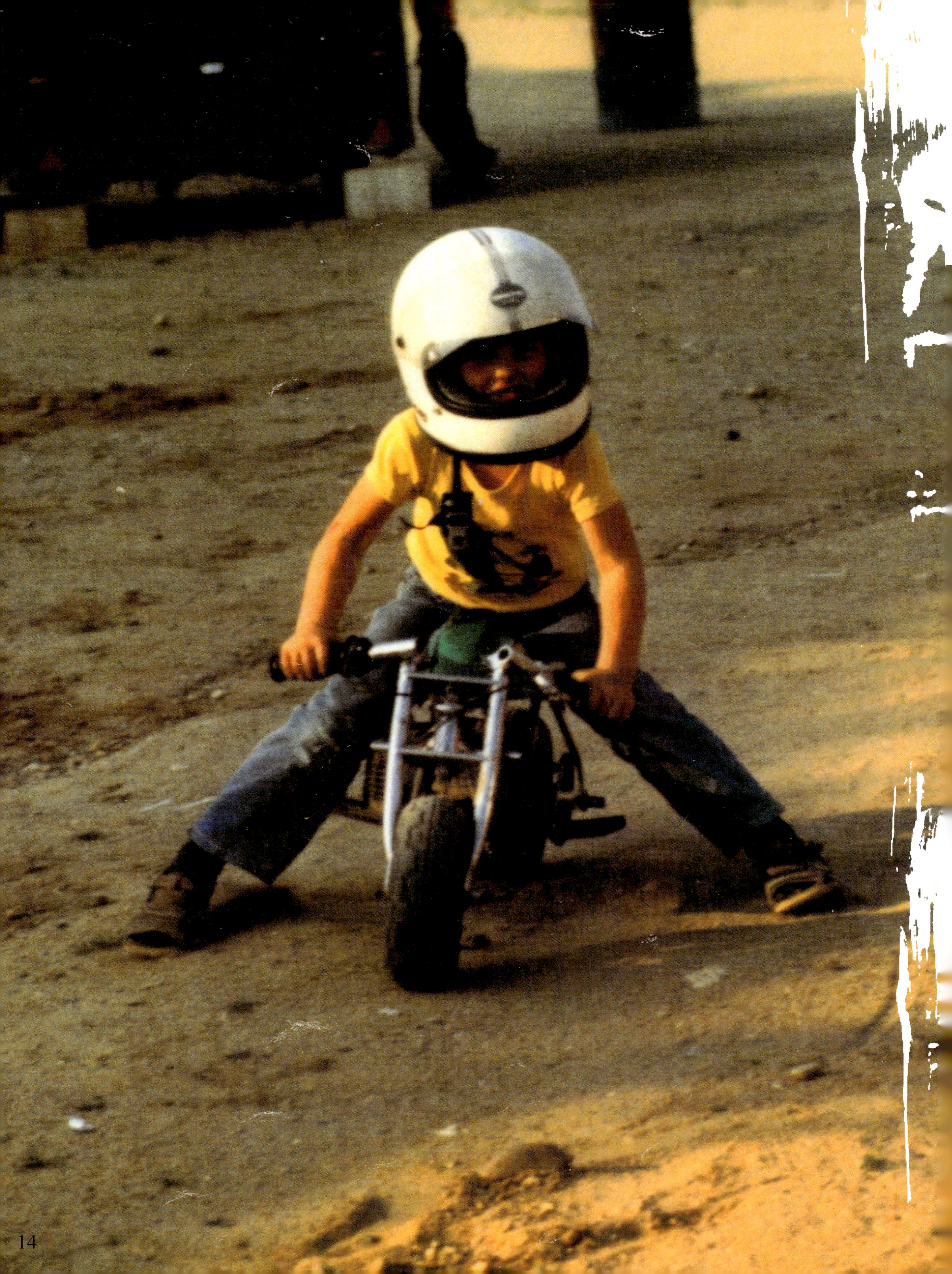

Wenn Vater Schumacher die Kerpener Kartbahn mit einem Besen sauberkehrte, band er sich ums linke Handgelenk eine Leine. An der Leine hing das Kinder-Kart mit Rasenmähermotor. Michael fuhr so weit die Leine reichte. Dann hatte er zu warten, bis der Vater besenschwingend aufholte. Kinder-Kart, Kinder-Motorrad, Sturzhelm im Kindergartenalter: Das war die Zeit, in der er sich auf alle seine späteren Gegner bereits zehn Jahre Vorsprung antrainierte.

When Schumacher's father swept the kart track in Kerpen, he tethered a line to his left wrist. Attached to the line was a child's kart powered by a lawnmower engine. Michael drove as far as the line would stretch, and then had to wait for his father to catch up. Child's kart, child's motorbike, helmet at kindergarten age: That was the time when Michael gained a ten year advantage over all other later rivals.

Mentre pulisce la pista da kart di Kerpen, papà Schumacher al polso sinistro tiene legato un ìguinzaglioì, e al guinzaglio è legato il minikart equipaggiato... con il motore per tosaerba. Michael va fin dove arriva il guinzaglio. Poi aspetta che il padre lo raggiunga. Minikart, minimoto, casco già in età d'asilo: è il periodo in cui Michael si assicura dieci anni di vantaggio sui suoi futuri avversari.

16

Michaels Kinderstube war die Kartbahn. Er hat weder Modelleisenbahn gespielt noch Indianer. Sein Spielzeug waren Slickreifen und Zahnräder. Er vergeudete keine Zeit mit übertriebener Schulbildung. Man lernt fürs Leben heißt es. Daher war ihm die Lehre der Bodenhaftung am wichtigsten.

Michael's playground was the karting track. He played neither cowboys and indians nor with a train set. His toys were slick tyres and gear wheels. He didn't squander his time on excessive schooling. They say you learn throughout life. And that's why, for him, lessons in road handling were most important.

La stanza dei giochi di Michael è la pista di kart. Non gioca né con i soldatini né col trenino. I suoi giocattoli sono le gomme slick e gli ingranaggi. A scuola non perde troppo tempo. Il proverbio recita: "non scholae sed vitae discimus". E quel che piú conta per lui è l'aderenza al fondo stradale.

Die Formel Ford bescherte Michael das erste Monoposto-Erlebnis, er wurde 1988 zweiter in der EM und vierter in der Deutschen Meisterschaft. Auf dem Salzburgring nahm er ein Regenrennen vom siebten Startplatz unter die Räder. Nach der ersten Runde lag er vorne, und es kam zu einer schicksalhaften Begegnung mit dem Rennstallbesitzer Willy Weber: „Genial, wie der Junge das Auto bewegte. Ich ließ ihn nachher kommen und war ein bißchen enttäuscht, denn einer, der so spielerisch schnell fuhr, konnte doch nicht so schüchtern sein…".

Formula Ford gave Michael his first monoposto experience - in 1988 he came second in the European Championship and fourth in the German Championship. On the Salzburgring, he started a rain race from seventh position. After the first round he was in front, and as fate would have it, also drew the attention of team owner Willy Weber: "How that youngster handled the car was brilliant! I asked him to join me afterwards and was a bit disappointed. How could someone who drives so naturally quick be so shy… "

La Formula Ford regala a Michael la prima esperienza su una monoposto; nel 1988 conquista il secondo posto nel Campionato europeo e il quarto posto nel Campionato tedesco. Sul Salzburgring, sotto la pioggia, parte in settima posizione; dopo il primo giro è in testa; incontra Willy Weber. E' l'incontro che segnerà il suo futuro: "Il modo in cui quel ragazzo teneva la vettura era semplicemente geniale. Lo mandai a chiamare, ma fui leggermente deluso: un ragazzo dalla guida così veloce non poteva essere così timido..."

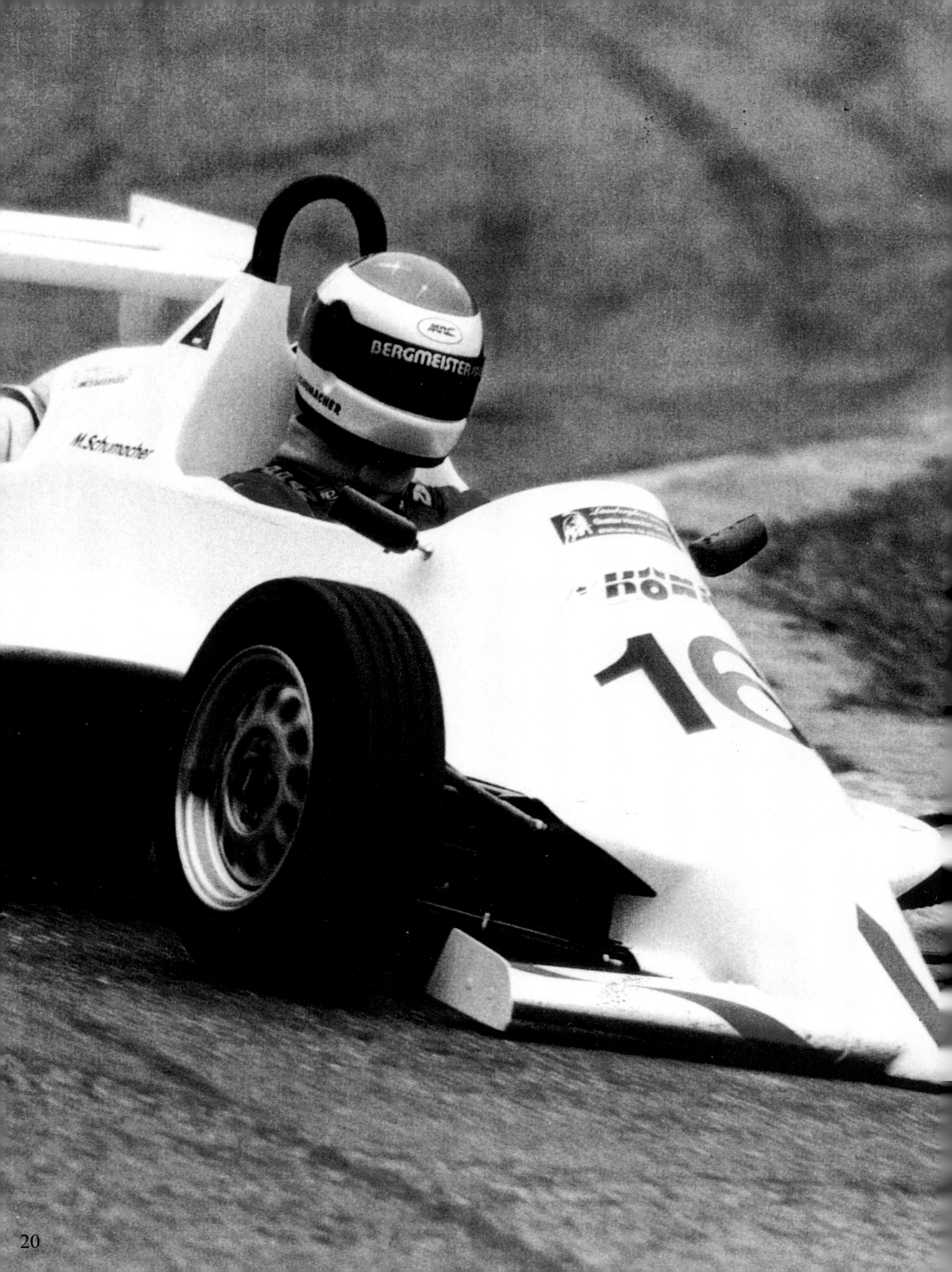
BERGMEISTER
M.Schumacher

Nachdem zwischen 1984 und 1987 drei Deutsche Kart-Meisterschaften gewonnen wurden, Michael 1985 Vizeweltmeister und 1986 dritter in der EM wurde, 1987 der Europameistertitel von dem 18jährigen eingefahren wurde, sponserte ein Lamborghini-Händler aus Landau 1988 die Formel König, wo er aus dem Stand mit dem 75-PS-Flitzer Deutscher Meister wurde. Bereits 1985 war Michael erstmals mit dem Rennfahrertod konfrontiert worden. Als Stefan Bellof, den er sehr gut kannte, in Belgien verunglückte, „machten wir drei Monate Pause", wie sich Jürgen Dilk erinnert.

After winning three German karting championships between 1984 and 1987, Michael became world championship runner-up in 1985, and took third in the 1986 European Championship. In 1987 the 18-year-old conquered the European Championship title, and was sponsored by a Lamborghini dealer from Landau in the 1988 Formula König, where he catapulted ahead to become German Champion in a 75 bhp sporty little job. In 1985 Michael was confronted for the first time with the death of a race driver. When Stefan Bellof, whom he knew very well, was killed in Belgium, "We took a three month break," remembers Jürgen Dilk.

Ai tre titoli di campione tedesco nel kart, conquistati tra il 1984 e il 1987, seguono il titolo di vicecampione del mondo nel 1985 e il terzo posto nel Campionato europeo del 1987. Nel 1988, un concessionario Lamborghini di Landau sponsorizza il 18enne Michael nella Formula König, nella quale alla prima uscita con il bolide da 75 cavalli vince il Campionato tedesco.

1989

FORMEL 3

1990

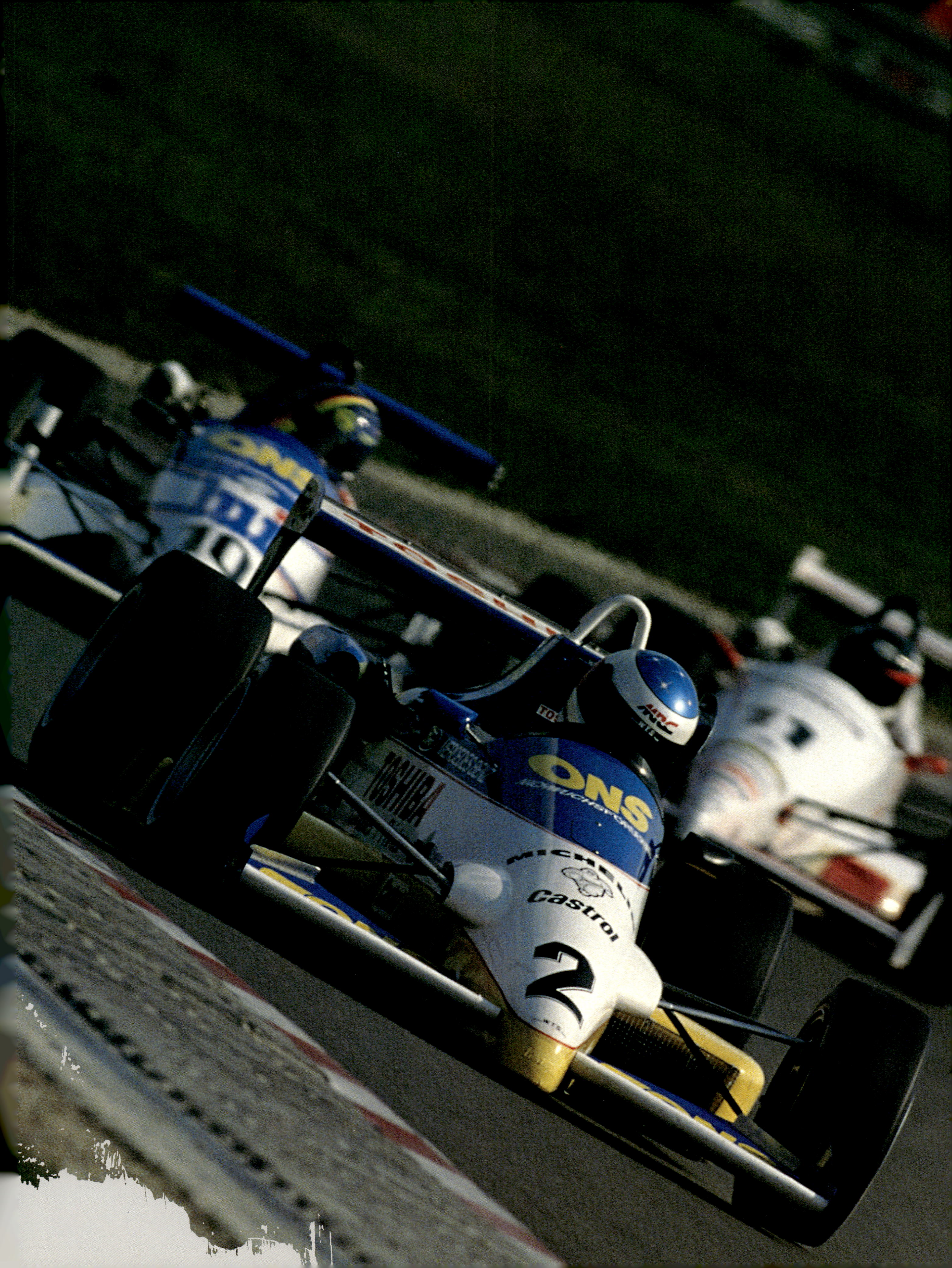
ONS
TOSHIBA
Castrol
2

Bei

rsten Test in Willy Webers Formel-3-Reynard war Michael „nach drei Runden 1,5 Sekunden hneller als mein Stammpilot Engstler", erinnert sich Weber. Michael bedauerte: „Ich hab' leider kein Geld". Darauf Weber: „Ich gebe Dir zwei Jahre, du mußt nur Gasgeben, den Rest erledige ich".

At the first test in Willy Weber's Formula 3 Reynard, Michael was "1.5 seconds faster than my regular pilot, Engstler, after just three laps," recalls Weber. Michael regretted that "unfortunately I have no money." Weber responded, "I'll give you two years. You just go flat-out, and leave the rest to me."

Al primo test sulla Reynard F3 di Willy Weber, Michael "già al terzo giro era piú veloce di un secondo e mezzo del pilota di casa Engstler", ricorda Weber. Michael è dispiaciuto: "Purtroppo mi mancano i soldi". Weber replica: "Ti dò due anni, tu pigia l'acceleratore, al resto penso io...".

Worauf hatte Willy Weber spekuliert? „Ich war ein Spieler, Michael hat mich beeindruckt", und so wurde 1989 jener nur zwei Papierseiten umfassende Vertrag geschlossen, der 1999 endet und eine Partnerschaft besiegelte, die sofort zum Höhenflug ansetzte und alle Prognosen über den Haufen warf. „In diesen zwei Formel-3-Jahren 1989 und 1990", sagt Willy Weber, „ist mir klar geworden, was in diesem Jungen wirklich steckt."

On what was Willy Weber speculating? "I was a gambler, and Michael impressed me." So in 1989 a two-page agreement was signed, to end in 1999, and sealed a partnership that immediately sky-rocketed and surpassed all expectations. "In the two Formula 3 years of 1989 and 1990," said Willy Weber, "the capabilities that lay in this young man became clear."

L'obiettivo di Willy Weber? "Personalmente mi sentivo come un giocatore d'azzardo, ma Michael mi aveva molto impressionato". E cosí, nel 1989, viene stipulato quel contratto di sole due pagine, la cui validità scade nel 1999, che sigilla una partnership dal successo strepitoso - un successo al di là di qualsiasi pronostico.

"Nelle due stagioni di Formula 3, il 1989/90", dice Weber, "mi resi conto che quel ragazzo possedeva veramente delle doti fuori dal comune."

27

"Er ist ein Siegertyp, der sich von Mädchen und Freunden nicht ablenken ließ. Michael realisierte von Anfang an, daß Rennen keine Betriebsausflüge sind..." (Willy Weber)

"He's a winning-type who doesn't allow himself to be distracted by girls nor friends. Michael realised at an early stage that racing isn't a joyride." (Willy Weber)

"Michael é un vincitore nato che non si lascia distogliere dalle ragazze o dalle compagnie. Sin dal principio aveva capito che le competizioni non sono delle gite aziendali." (Willy Weber)

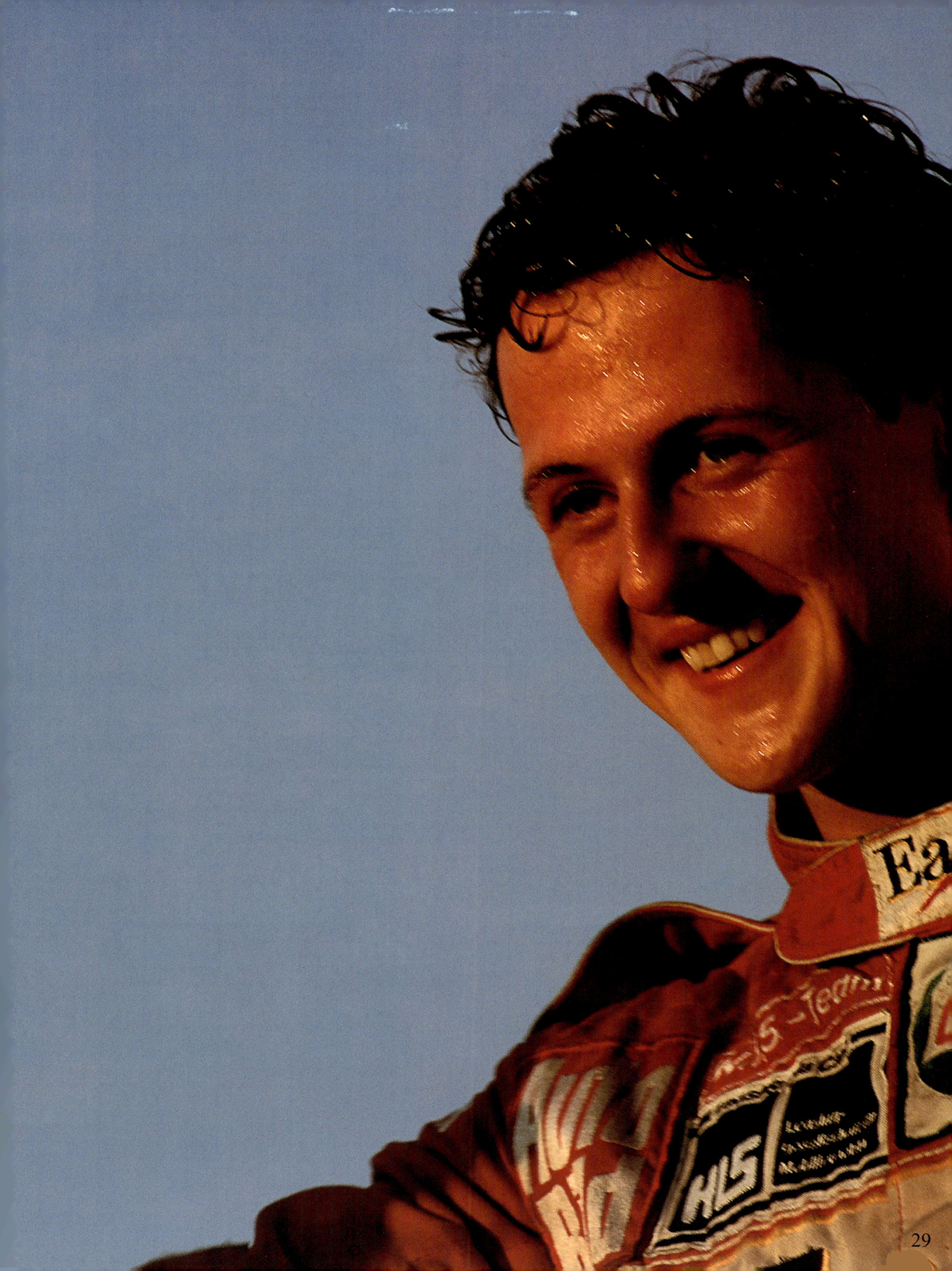
HLS

Die Eltern, die Kart-Bahn, die Kantine sowie „Schnitzel und Fritten waren bis 17 das Leben des Michael", weiß Jürgen Dilk. Vater Rolf, (unten mit Ralf und Michael), ein gelernter Feuerungsmaurer, war für die Kerpener Kart-Bahn verantwortlich. Die Mutter - vor ihrer Gaststätte mit den Jungs - packte für jedes Rennen 40 Schnitzel als Marschverpflegung ein...

His parents, the kart track, the canteen, as well as "schnitzel and chips were Michael's life until he was 17-years-old," reminisces Jürgen Dilk. Father Rolf (below with Ralf and Michael), a trained fireplace builder, was responsible for the kart track in Kerpen. His mother - in front of her restaurant with the boys - packed 40 schnitzels as field rations for every race.

I genitori, la pista da kart, la mensa, così come "le bistecche e le patatine fritte fino a 17 anni erano tutto il mondo di Michael" racconta Jürgen Dilk. Papà Rolf (sotto, insieme a Ralf e Michael), esperto in strutture antincendio, è responsabile della pista da kart di Kerpen. La madre - davanti alla piccola trattoria con i ragazzi - prepara per ogni gara una quarantina di bistecche come provvista...

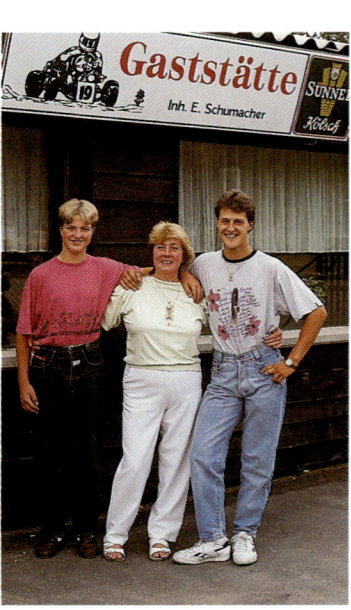

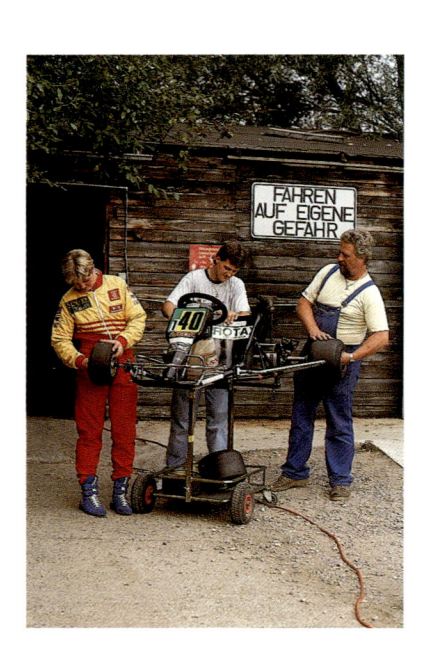

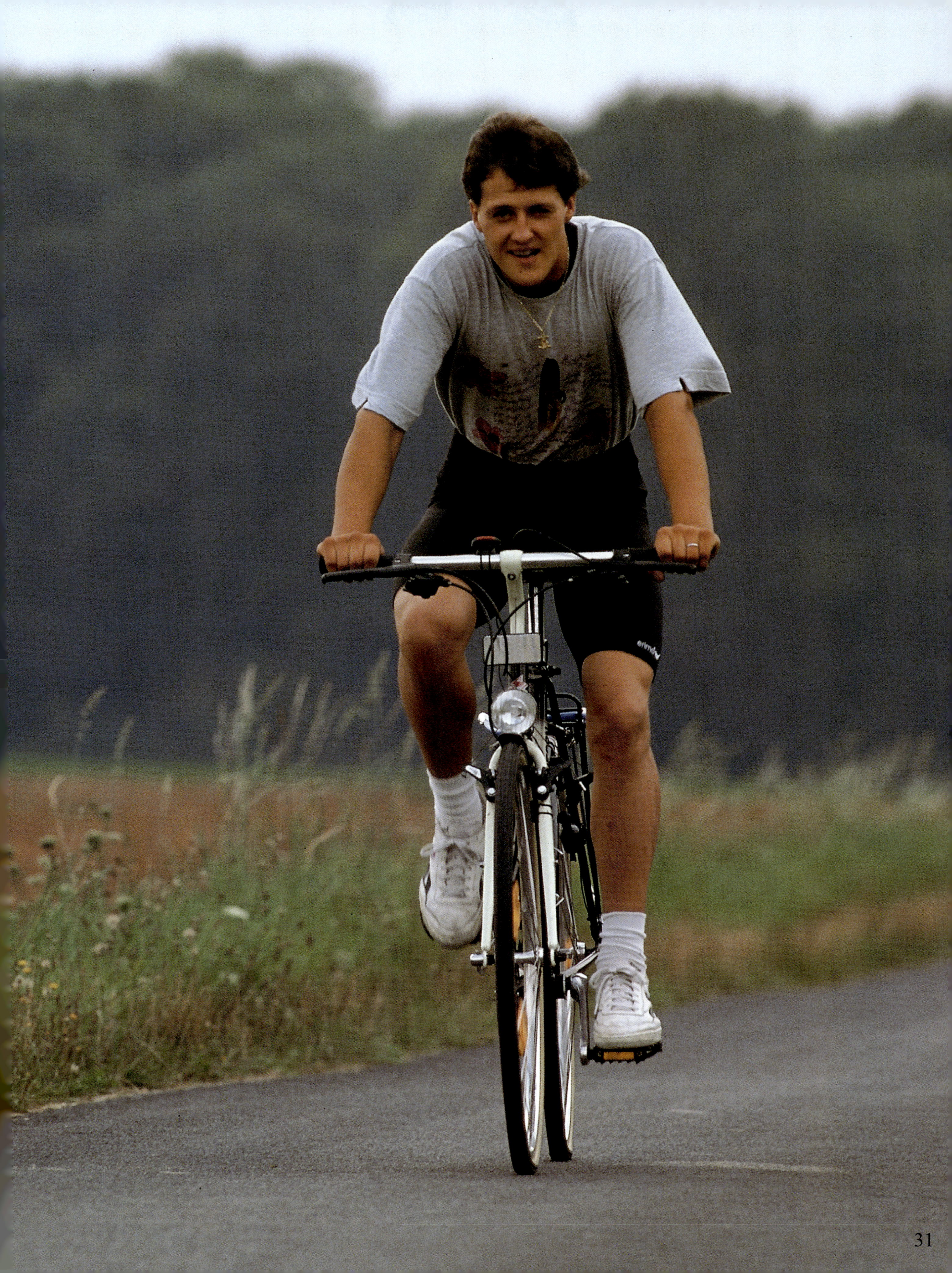

Jürgen Dilk (hier oben mit Michael an den Niagara-Fällen) ist seine erste Aufstiegshilfe. Der Automaten-Techniker aus [...] Erklärung, daß er an Vaters statt Proteste für den zehnjährigen Michael einlegen darf. Als Dilk den Sportlehrer Peter St[...] davon. Der Trainer mußte beim Lauftraining zum Fahrrad greifen... Michaels Lehrstelle als Kfz-Mechaniker bei der Fir[...] Einmal fehlten 500 Mark für Reifen. Michael bastelte sich eine Notlüge: „Ein Metzger borgt mir das Geld...". Jürgen D[...] Wirklichkeit holte sich Michael die Reifen aus der Mülltonne. Und gewann das Rennen.

Jürgen Dilk (above with Michael at Niagara Falls), was the first to help Schumi on his rise to the top. The gaming machin[...] that he was allowed to lodge protests on behalf of 10-year-old Michael's father. When Dilk engaged the fitness trainer [...] him. When Michael ran, the instructor rode a bicycle alongside... Michael's apprenticeship as a car mechanic at the Be[...] 500 Marks for some tyres. Michael spun a white lie: "A butcher lent me the money..." Jürgen Dilk, today the President [...] taken the tyres out of a rubbish container. He won the race.

Jürgen Dilk (qui in alto, con Michael alle cascate del Niagara) è il primo appoggio della carriera. Tecnico per distributo[...] sitata una dichiarazione ufficiale che lo autorizza a inoltrare, in vece del padre, i reclami per Michael (che all'epoca ha [...] già un mese dopo getta la spugna: Michael lo stacca continuamente, per il footing l'allenatore deve usare la bicicletta. [...] finiva la settimana lavorativa, avendo cose tempo libero per le gare di kart." Una volta gli mancano 500 marchi per le go[...] ufficiale dei tifosi di Schumacher, in guell' occasione disse: "Bene, allora possiamo correre, vero?..." In realtà Michael [...]

rf nahm seinen Sohn Guido und Michael zu den Kart-Rennen mit. Von der Stadt Kerpen bekam Dilk eine eidesstattliche
erk engagierte, um die Kondition der Jungs zu heben, warf der Trainer nach vier Wochen das Handtuch: Michael lief ihm
rgmeister war - so Dilk - „ein Glücksgriff, denn er bekam ab Donnerstag für die Kart-Rennen frei".
eute Präsident des 1. offiziellen Michael Schumacher-Fan Club, damals: „Na, dann können wir doch noch fahren…". In

nician from Alsdorf took his son Guido and Michael to the kart races. Dilk received a declaration from the city of Kerpen
Stollenwerk to improve the boys' stamina, the trainer threw in the towel after just four weeks: Michael was far ahead of
ter firm was, says Dilk "a godsend. His week finished Thursday leaving him free for the kart races". Once he was short
first official Michael Schumacher Fan Club, said at that time: "Well then, we can still drive..." In reality, Michael had

matici, nativo di Alsdorf, Dilk accompagna il figlio Guido e Michael alle gare di kart. Al comune di Kerpen viene depo-
anni). Dilk incarica Peter Stollenwerk, insegnante di educazione fisica, di curare la preparazione dei ragazzi, ma questi
o di apprendista meccanico alla ditta Bergmeister, racconta Dilk, "fu per Michael un colpo di fortuna, perché il giovedì
per necessità, Michael ripiega su una bugia: "i soldi me li presta un macellaio" … Jürgen Dilk, presidente del primo club
e le gomme dalla spazzatura e vince.

1990 1991

GRUPPE C

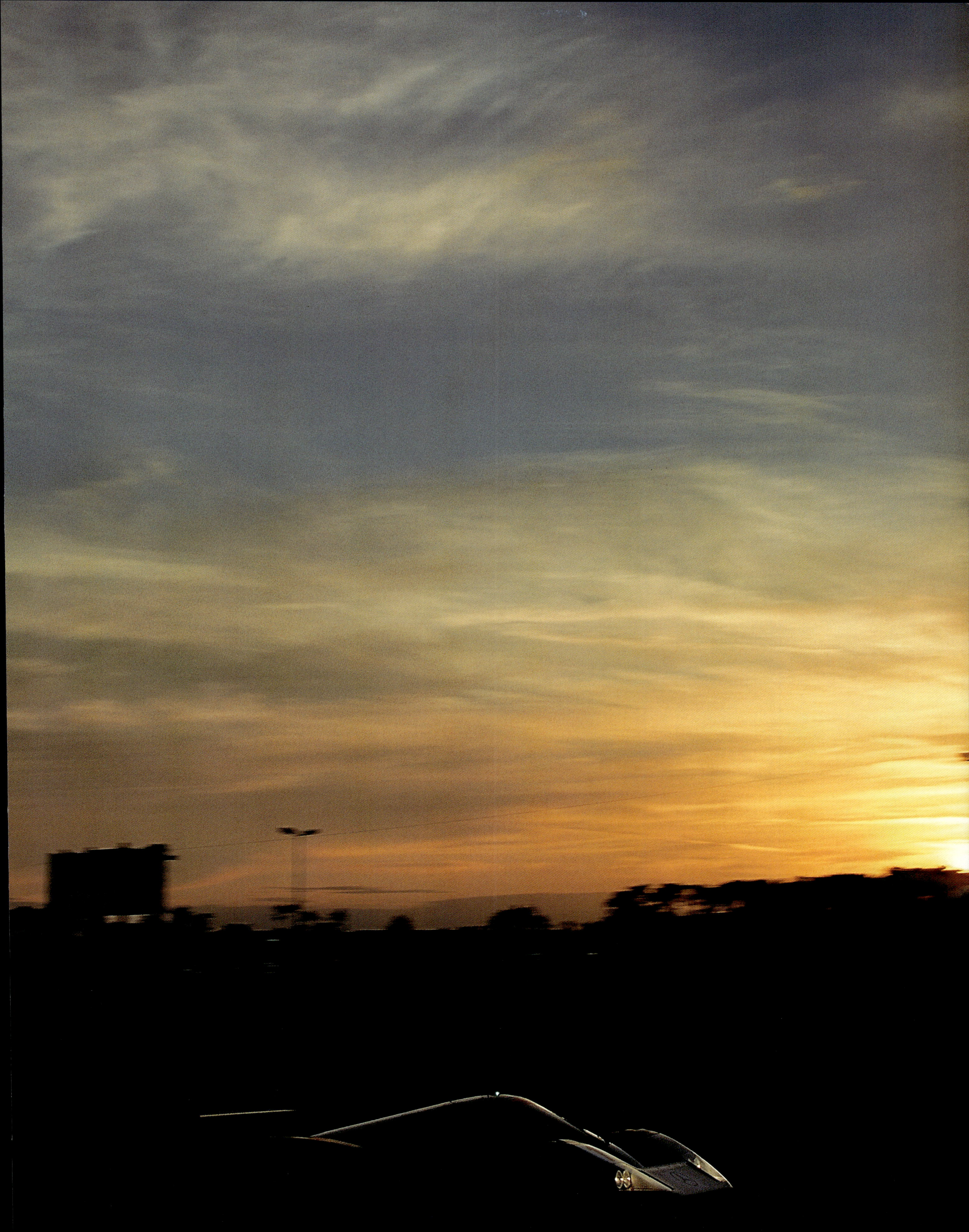

Die Formel 1 stand noch in den Sternen, auch wenn sie Willy Weber schon im Fernrohr sah, als Jochen Neerpasch den Michael 1990 in das Gruppe-C-Team von Sauber-Mercedes-Benz holte, wo der Rohdiamant seinen Schliff in Outfit und Sprache bekam.

Formula 1 was still far off in Michael's future, but Willy Weber was already a fortune teller. At this time, in 1990, Jochen Neerpasch took Michael into the Group C team of Sauber Mercedes-Benz. Here the rough diamond became polished in dress and language.

La Formula 1 è ancora lontana anni luce, ma Willy Weber la intravede al telescopio: nel 1990, Jochen Neerpasch chiama Michael al team Sauber/Mercedes-Benz nel Gruppo C, nel quale il diamante ancora grezzo viene... tagliato per la prima volta per le uscite in pubblico.

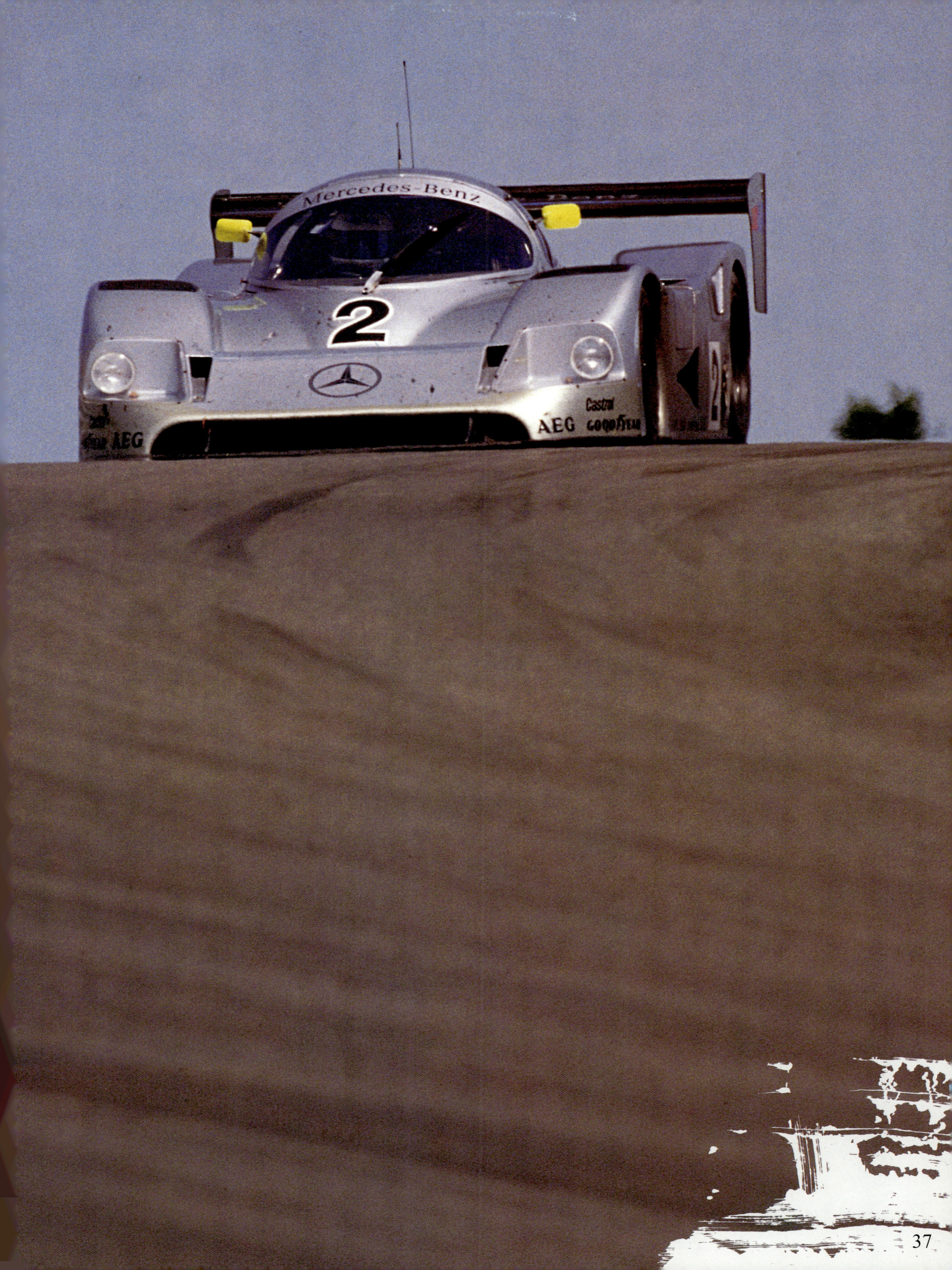
Mercedes-Benz
2
AEG
Castrol
GOODYEAR

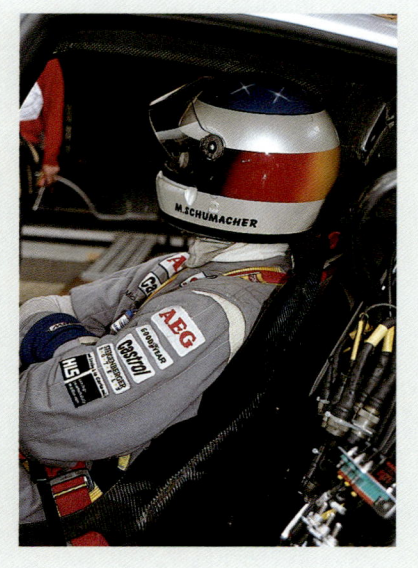

„Vom ersten Tag an", erinnert sich Peter Sauber, „haben wir nicht gedacht, er sei ein Überflieger. Aber er hatte ein unglaubliches Fahrgefühl und war in der Verfolgung eines Ziels hartnäckiger als Heinz-Harald Frentzen und Karl Wendlinger." Frentzen fiel laut Peter Sauber „als sehr schnell auf, Schumacher war mehr der Draufgänger und Wendlinger der Ruhige."

"From the first test on," remembers Peter Sauber, "we didn't think he was such a high-flyer. But he had an incredible instinct for driving, and in his pursuit of a goal he was even more determined than Heinz-Harald Frentzen and Karl Wendlinger." Frentzen stood apart from the rest said Sauber, "as very fast, whereas Schumacher was more the daredevil, and Wendlinger was the quiet one."

"Ai primi test", ricorda Peter Sauber, "non pensavamo che avrebbe fatto una carriera folgorante. Ma nella guida mostrava un'incredibile sensibilità, e nel perseguire i propri obiettivi era più caparbio di Heinz-Harald Frentzen e di Karl Wendlinger."
Secondo Peter Sauber, "Frentzen si metteva in evidenza per la velocità, Schumacher per la grinta, Wendlinger era il più tranquillo."

NISSAN
JOEST
Mercedes-Benz
2
AEG
NISSAN

AEG
Castrol
GOODYEAR

HYDRO
W S
P C
France
NISSAN

Shell Shell Shell Shell
Mercedes-Benz
2

SCHUMACHER BOSS

Mercedes-Benz
J.MASS
M.SCHUMACHER

Mercedes-Benz
2
AEG
Castrol

CAMPARI ESSO ESSO

Michaels Talent offenbarte sich, als er mit Jochen Mass auf dem C9 gegen die Stars Baldi/Schlesser fuhr. Er war nicht nur der Schnellste, er verbrauchte dabei auch den wenigsten Sprit und schonte sogar die Reifen.

Michael's talent became obvious after he drove with Jochen Mass in a C9 against aces Baldi/Schlesser. He was not only the fastest - he used the least amount of fuel and even preserved his tyres.

Il talento di Michael si rivela appieno quando con Jochen Mass gareggia sulla C9 contro le star Baldi/Schlesser. Schumacher non solo risulta il più veloce, ma consuma meno di tutti e risparmia perfino le gomme.

Am Norisring traf Michael die Mercedes-Legenden Karl Kling, Juan Manuel Fangio, Hans Herrmann und Eugen Böhringer. Und im 3-Liter-Kompressor Mercedes des Jahres 1939 nahm er seinen ersten Unterricht in Grand-Prix-Geschichte...

At the Norisring Michael met Mercedes legends Karl Kling, Juan Manuel Fangio, Hans Herrmann and Eugen Böhringer. And in a 3-litre compressor 1939 Mercedes he experienced his first lesson in the history of Grand Prix.

Al Norisring di Norimberga, Michael incontra Karl Kling, Juan Manuel Fangio, Hans Herrmann e Eugen Böhringer, i grandi miti della Mercedes. Sulla Mercedes tre litri con compressore del 1939 vive la prima lezione di storia dei Gran Premi...

43

FORMEL 1

1991

ab

1991

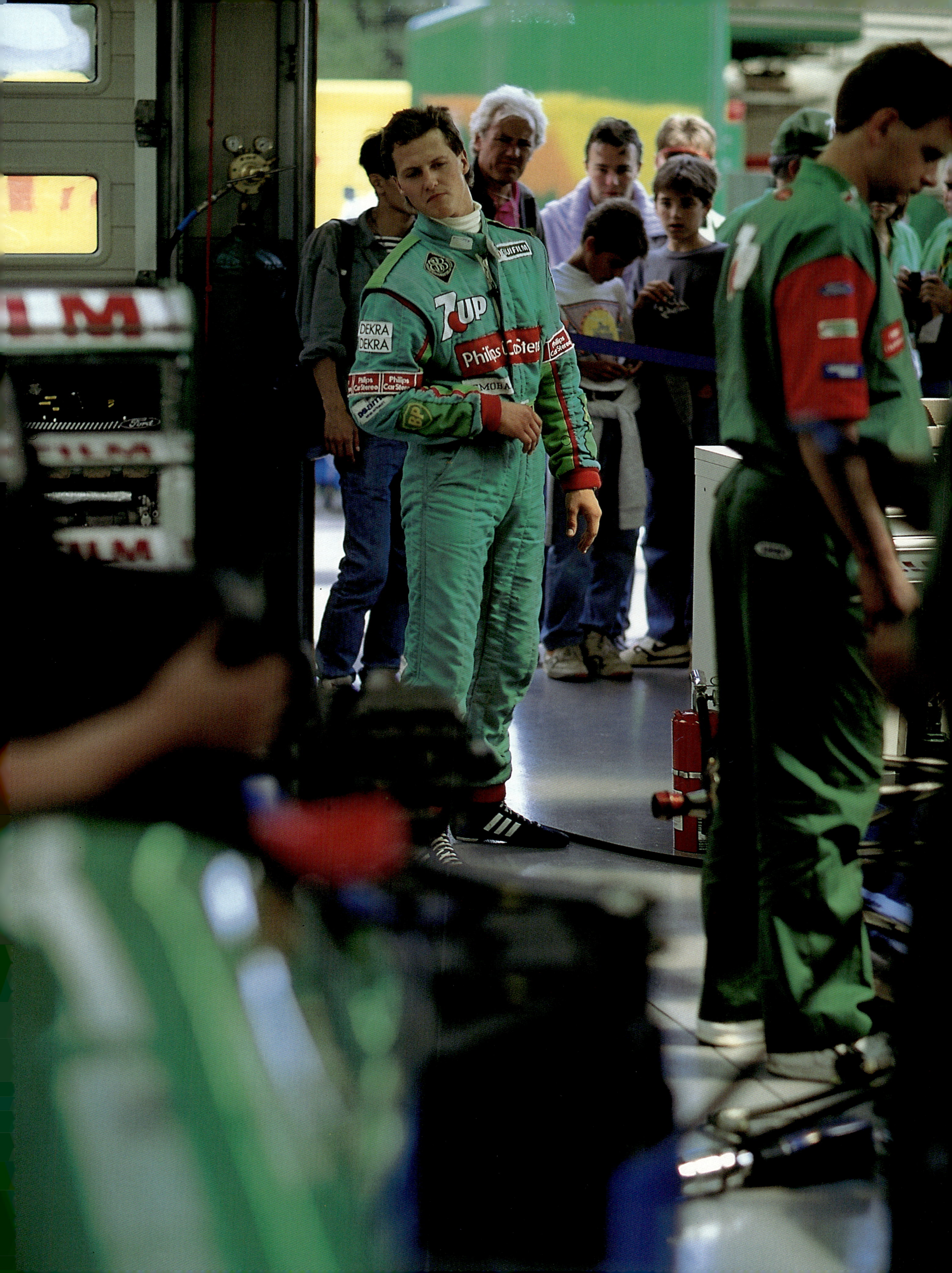
7UP
DEKRA
DEKRA

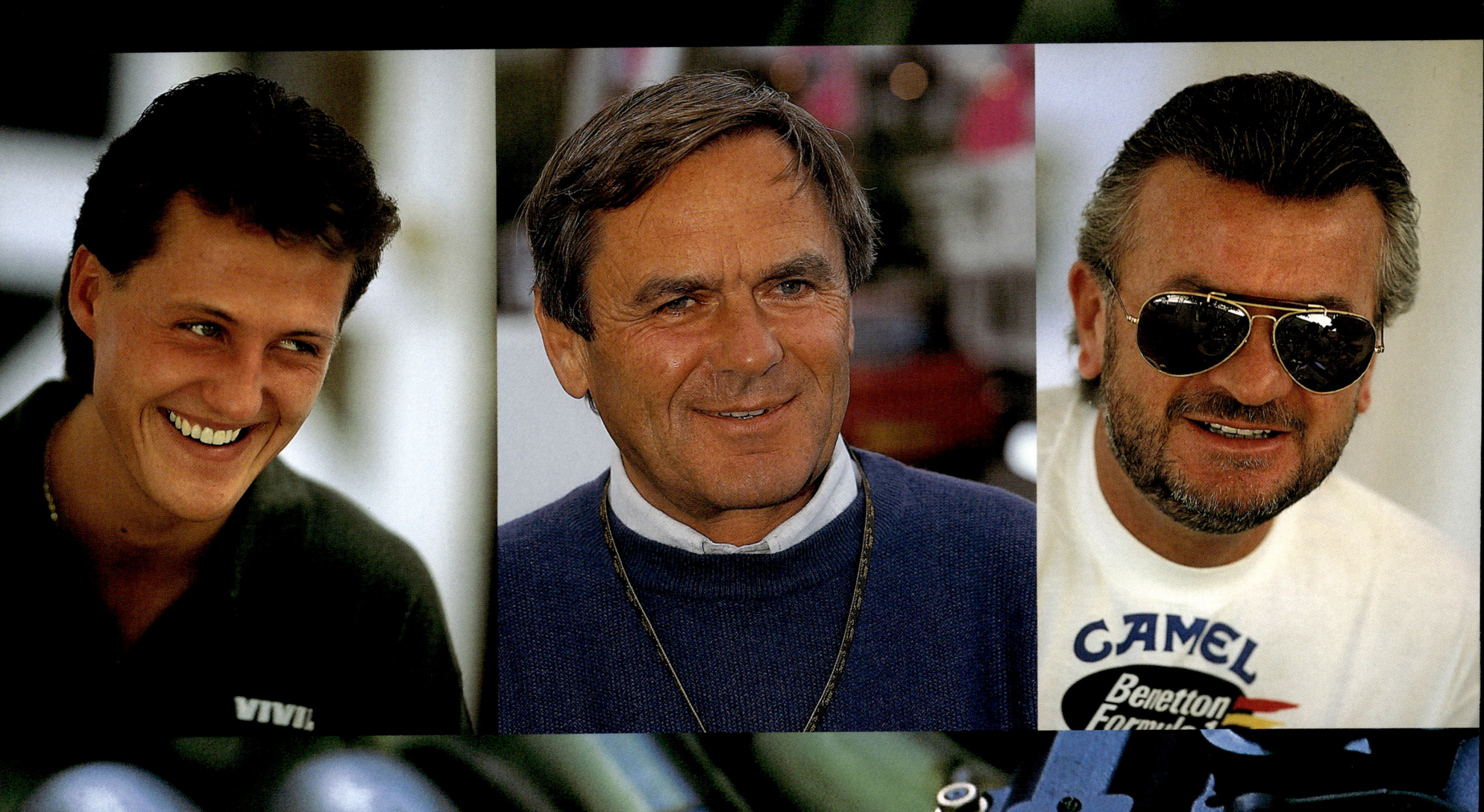

Die Bankgarantie über 80.000 Pfund, die Eddie Jordan für Schumi
auch wenn sie letztlich nicht angetastet wurde. Die Jordan-Fahrk
eiste Jochen Neerpasch (Mitte) von Mercedes-Benz los, DEKRA s

Willy Weber (above right) produced a bank guarantee for £80,
although it was never needed. A driving ticket for Jordan for the
from Jochen Neerpasch (middle) of Mercedes-Benz, and DEKRA t

Willy Weber (in alto a destra) fornisce la garanzia bancaria di
Schumi... la somma non verrà toccata. Il biglietto della Jordan p
vengono messi a disposizione dalla Mercedes-Benz tramite Joche

rsten Formel-1-Test forderte, erbrachte Willy Weber (oben rechts),
e für den Belgien Grand Prix 1991 kostete 450.000 Mark, 300.000
ß 100.000 Mark zu.

, that Eddie Jordan required for Schumi's first Formula 1 test,
991 Belgian Grand Prix cost 450,000 deutschmarks. 300,000 came
w in another 100,000.

mila sterline che Eddie Jordan chiede per il primo test in F1 di
l Gran Premio del Belgio del 1991 costa 450mila marchi: 300mila
eerpasch (al centro), la DEKRA ne aggiunge altri 100mila.

Als Nigel Mansell am 23. August 1991 während des Freitag-Trainings in Spa-Francorchamps einen Blick auf den Zeitmonitor riskierte, fand er einen Namen, den er nicht kannte: „Shoemaker? Wer ist das?" Als Shoemaker den sensationellen siebten Startplatz okkupierte, wußte er mehr..

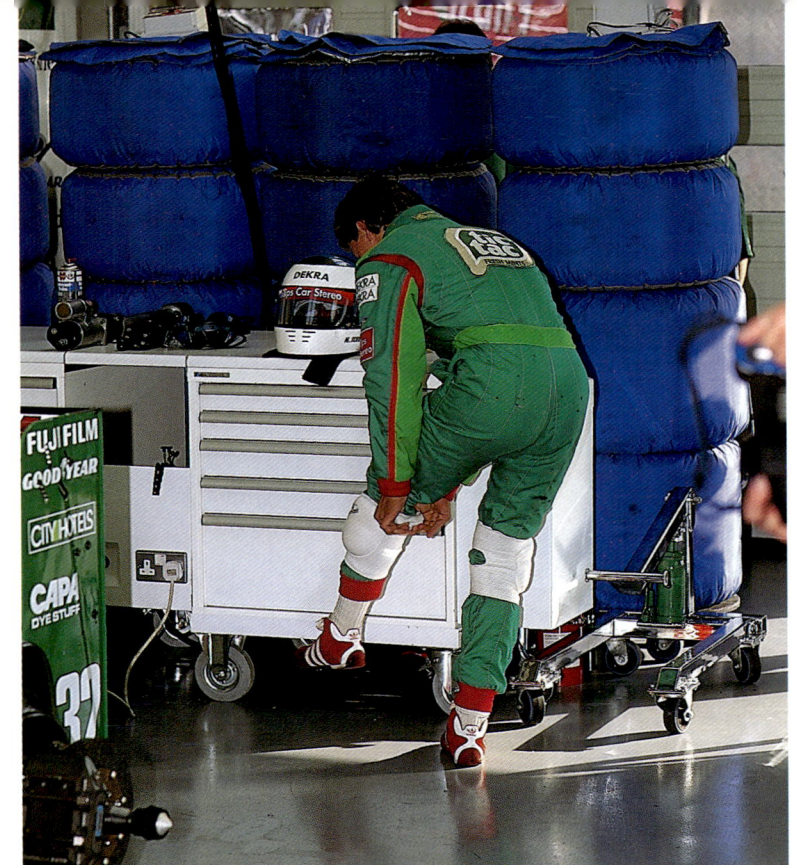

On 23 August 1991 during Friday's qualification in Spa-Francorchamps, Nigel Mansell cast an eye over the monitor and found an unfamiliar name: "Shoemaker? Who's that?" After Shoemaker took up seventh starting position, he knew more....

Venerdí 23 agosto 1991: durante le prove a Spa-Francorchamps, Nigel Mansell dà un'occhiata al monitor con i tempi e legge un nome sconosciuto: "Shoemaker? Chi è?" Quando tale Shoemaker conquista un sensazionale settimo posto nella griglia di partenza, ne sa già qualcosina di piú…

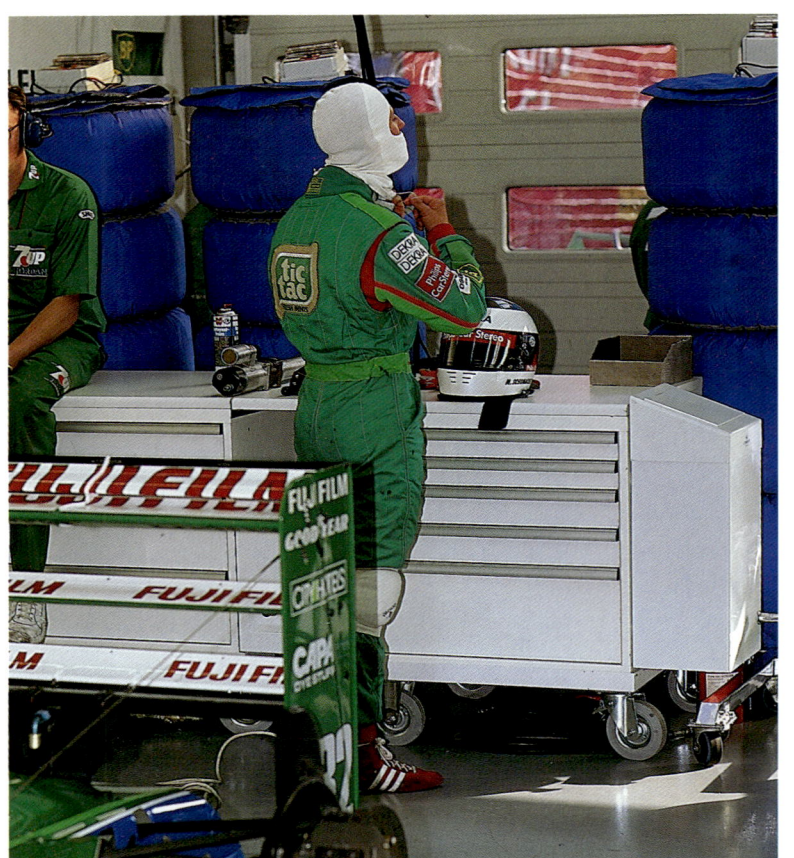

48

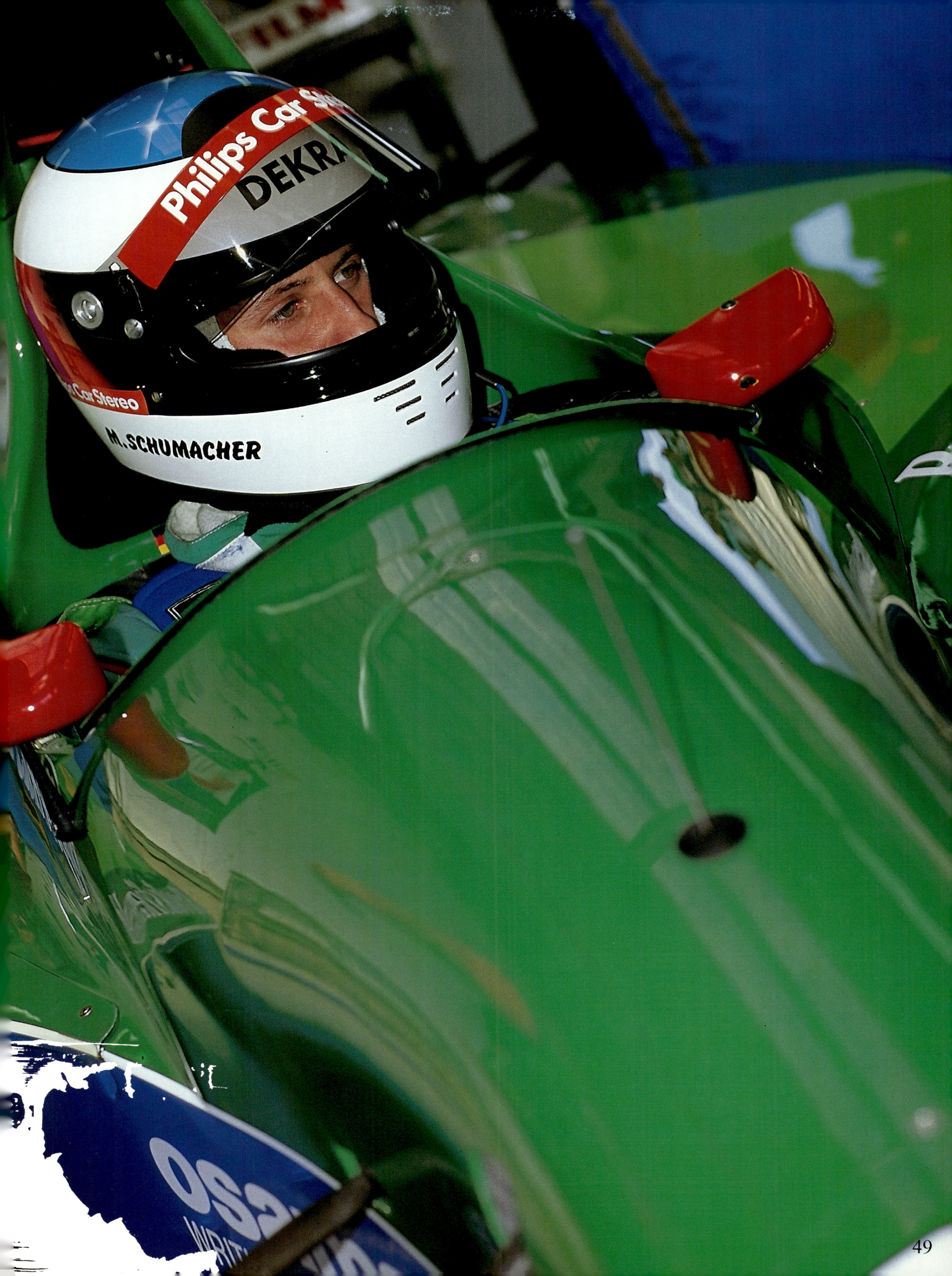
Philips Car Stereo
DEKRA
Car Stereo
M.SCHUMACHER

CAMEL
sparco
CAMEL
Reporter parfum
Diavia
SANYO
sparco
LISTA
Ford
Mobil
19
UNITED COLORS OF BENETTON
VIVIL
Ford
Diavia

In Belgien hatte Michael zusammen mit Willy Weber in einer Jugendherberge geschlafen. Trotzdem er am Start mit Kupplungsdefekt ausfiel, wollte er bei Jordan weitermachen. Jochen Neerpasch wußte aber schon, daß Jordan seine Ford-Motoren verlieren wird, daher transferierte er Schumi gegen dessen Willen zu Benetton - was sich in Monza zu einer riesigen Affäre ausweitete, weil Benetton erst seinen Fahrer Moreno in die Wüste schicken mußte.

In Belgium Michael and Willy Weber slept in a youth hostel. Despite retiring shortly after the start with a clutch defect, he still wanted to continue with Jordan. Jochen Neerpasch already knew that Jordan would lose their Ford engines, therefore he transferred Schumi, against his will, to Benetton - which turned into a huge affair in Monza - Benetton first had to send their driver, Moreno, packing.

In Belgio, insieme a Willy Weber, Michael pernotta in un ostello della gioventú. Benché un problema alla frizione lo costringa al ritiro già in partenza, è deciso a continuare con la Jordan. Ma Jochen Neerpasch, venuto a sapere che le forniture di motori Ford alla Jordan sarebbero cessate, trasferisce Schumi (contro la sua volontà) alla Benetton: un passaggio clamoroso dato che la squadra italiana deve dare il benservito al proprio pilota Moreno.

In Monza wurde die Startnummer 19, Schumacher auf Benetton-Ford, fünfter, was für Luciano Benetton - hier mit Michael - ein Festmahl war. Der Einlauf hieß Mansell-Senna-Prost-Berger-Schumacher-Piquet. „Da fuhren noch richtige Weltmeister mit, und keine Pappheinis wie heute", konstatierte Willy Weber.

Schumacher with starting number 19 came fifth in Monza in the Benetton Ford. For Luciano Benetton - here with Michael - this was a feast. In order of finishing: Mansell, Senna, Prost, Berger, Schumacher, Piquet. "That was when real world champions competed, and not the cardboard cut-outs of today," remarked Weber.

A Monza, il numero 19 Schumacher su Benetton-Ford si classifica quinto: per Luciano Benetton (qui con Michael) una vera festa. L'ordine d'arrivo recita: Mansell, Senna, Prost, Berger, Schumacher, Piquet. "Era un periodo in cui scendevano in pista tanti grandi nomi, campioni del mondo…", constata Willy Weber.

Marlboro
HONDA
COURTAULDS

FORMULA ONE SERVICE
Agip

Benetton Formula 1

VIVIL
USEN 440

Bei Benetton sollte Michael den dreifachen Weltmeister Nelson Piquet aufwecken, der das Potential des Autos nur noch rundenweise ausschöpfte...

At Benetton Michael put the pressure on triple world champion Nelson Piquet, who could really only utilise the car's full potential over several laps.

In casa Benetton si vuole che Michael dia uno scossone al tre volte campione del mondo Nelson Piquet, che all'epoca sfrutta appieno il potenziale della vettura solo per qualche giro...

UNITED COLORS
OF BENETTON

UNITED COLORS
OF BENETTON
SANYO
Mobil
M.Schumacher

UNITED COLORS

UNITED COLORS
OF BENETTON.

Power By
Ford
Mobil 1
UNITED COLORS
OF BENETTON.
VIVIL
USEN
440
GOODYEAR
SCHUMACHER

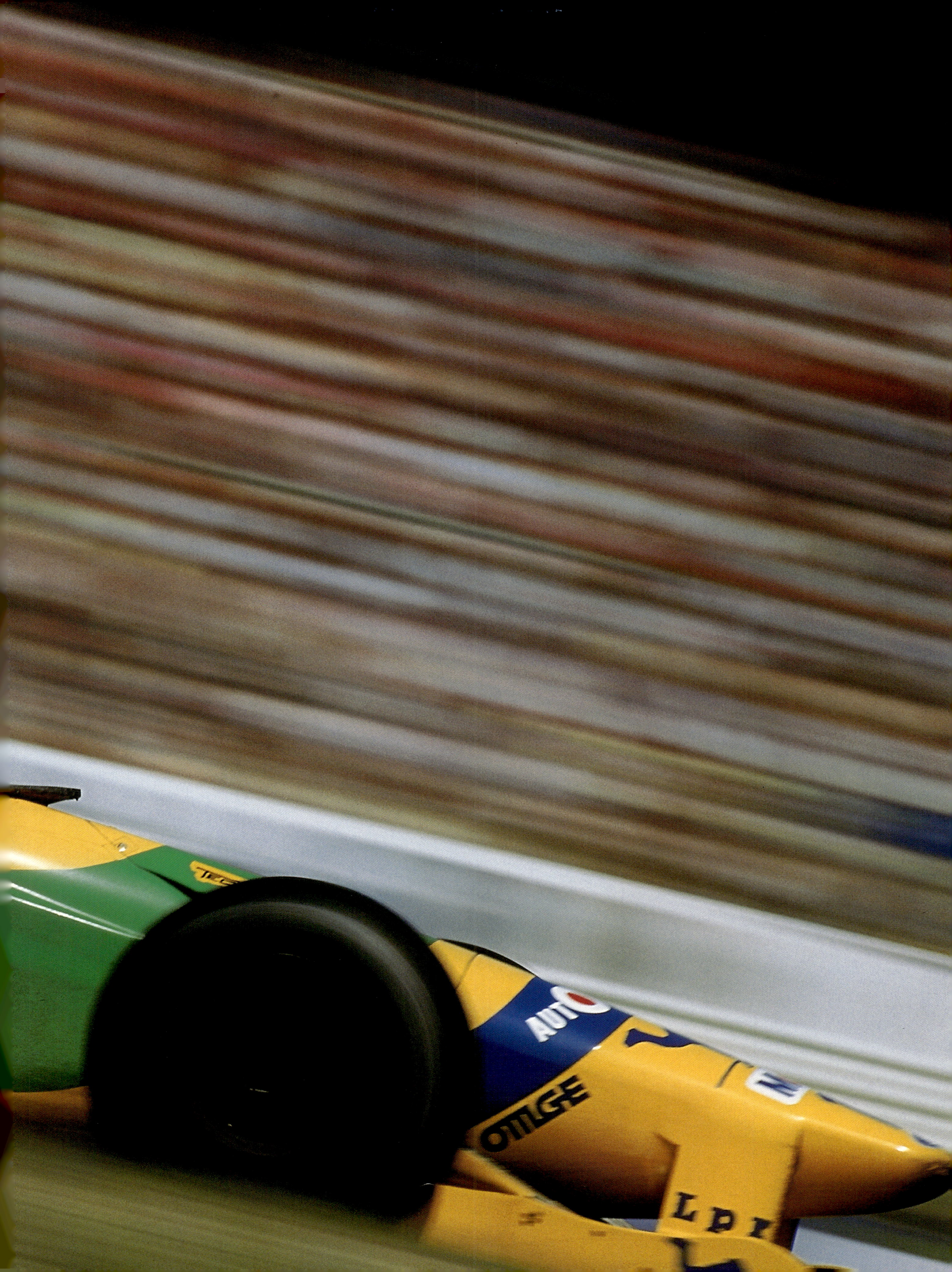

30. August 1992: Erster Grand-Prix-Sieg in Belgien. „Das Schöne an diesem Sieg", sagte Michael, „niemand hat ihn mir geschenkt, die Williams sind nicht vor mir ausgefallen und auch der Senna nicht!"

30th August 1992: First Grand Prix win in Belgium. "The wonderful thing about this victory," said Michael, "was that it wasn't handed to me on a platter. Williams didn't retire, and neither did Senna!"

Belgio, 30 agosto 1992: arriva la prima vittoria in un Gran Premio. "Il bello di quella vittoria", dice Michael, "è che nessuno me l'ha regalata, le Williams non si sono ritirate e Senna neppure!"

AUTOPOLIS
UNITED COLORS OF BENETTON

GOODYEAR
SANYO
Mobil
AUTOPOLIS
UNITED COLORS OF BENETTON
M.Schumacher

GOODYEAR
AUTOPOLIS
UNITED COLORS OF BENETTON
AMPS 1992

UNITED COLORS OF BENETTON
M.Schumacher

GOODYEAR
MOET

GOODYEAR
MOET
Labatt's
CHAMPION
Nigel Mansell

MOET
SANYO
Mobil
MOET & CHANDON

Momente wie diesen, den Sieg in Portugal 1993, pflegt Michael in seinem Tagebuch zu speichern. Das gewonnene Duell gegen Alain Prost auf Williams, der in diesem Jahr Weltmeister wurde, machte seinen zweiten Grand-Prix-Sieg noch wertvoller als seinen ersten in Spa, „speziell nach einem Wochenende, wo du keinen Pfifferling auf einen solchen Erfolg setzt."

Moments like this - the Portugal win in 1993 - are usually written in Michael's diary. Winning the duel against Williams pilot Alain Prost, who then went on to become world champion, made Schumi's second Grand Prix victory even more precious than his first in Spa, "especially after such a weekend. I didn't imagine, even in my wildest dreams, that I could win."

Momenti come quello della vittoria in Portogallo nel 1993 sono momenti che Michael abitualmente "memorizza" nel suo diario. Il duello con Alain Prost sulla Williams, che in quell'anno conquisterà il mondiale, rende ancor piú preziosa la sua seconda vittoria in un Gran Premio dopo quella di Spa, "soprattutto in un fine settimana in cui non punteresti un centesimo sul successo."

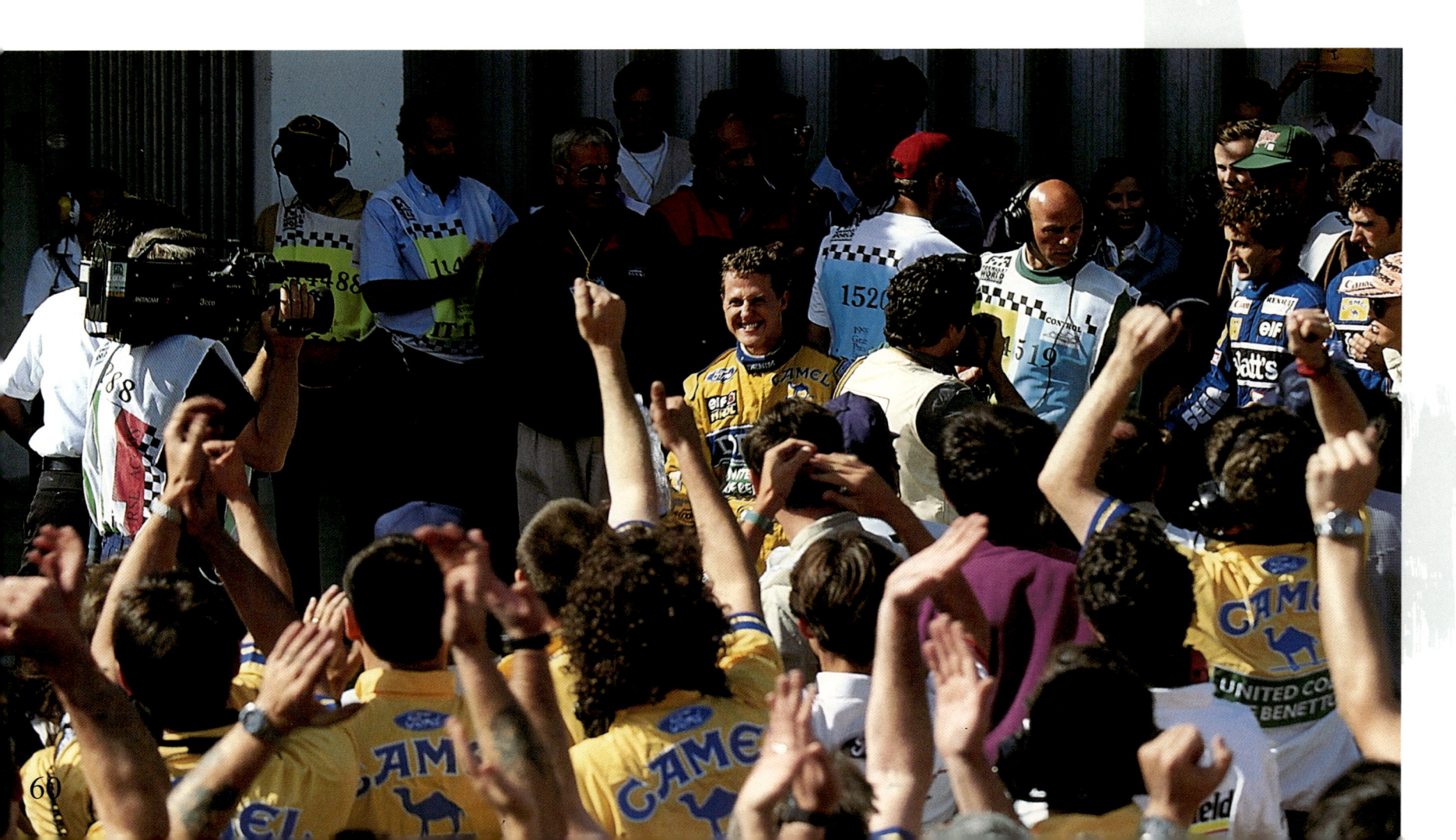

61

Das Verhältnis zu Ayrton Senna „war nicht besonders eng", offenbarte Michael, „seinen Respekt zu erlangen, war für mich etwas ganz Besonderes."

The relationship to Ayrton Senna "was not particularly close," admits Michael. "To earn his respect was very special to me."

I rapporti con Ayrton Senna "non sono mai stati particolarmente stretti", ricorda Michael, "conquistare la sua stima per me rappresentava qualcosa di veramente particolare".

Rothmans
Marlboro
MILD SEVEN
RENAULT
elf
MILD SEVEN
MILD SEVEN

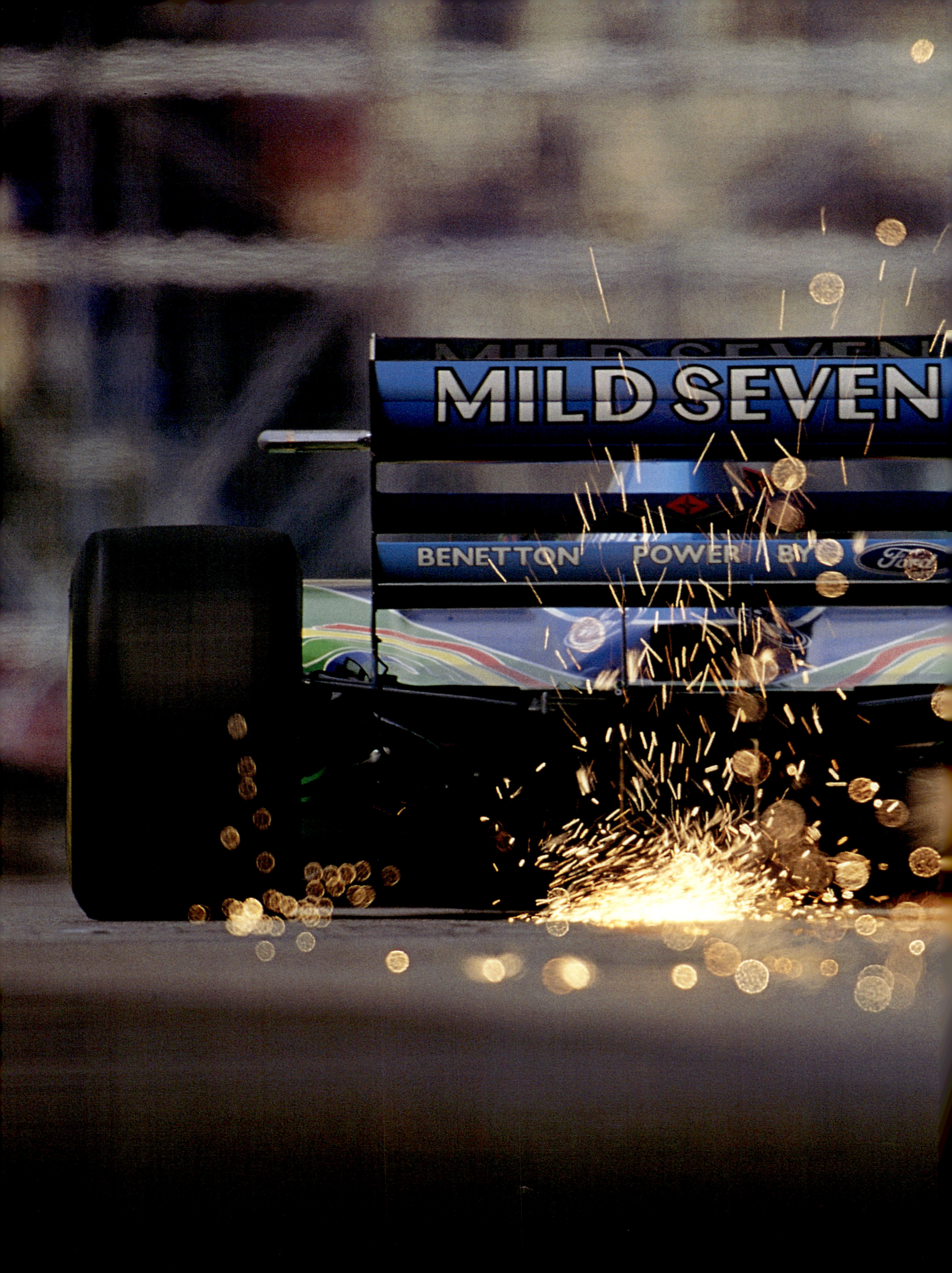
MILD SEVEN
BENETTON POWER BY Ford

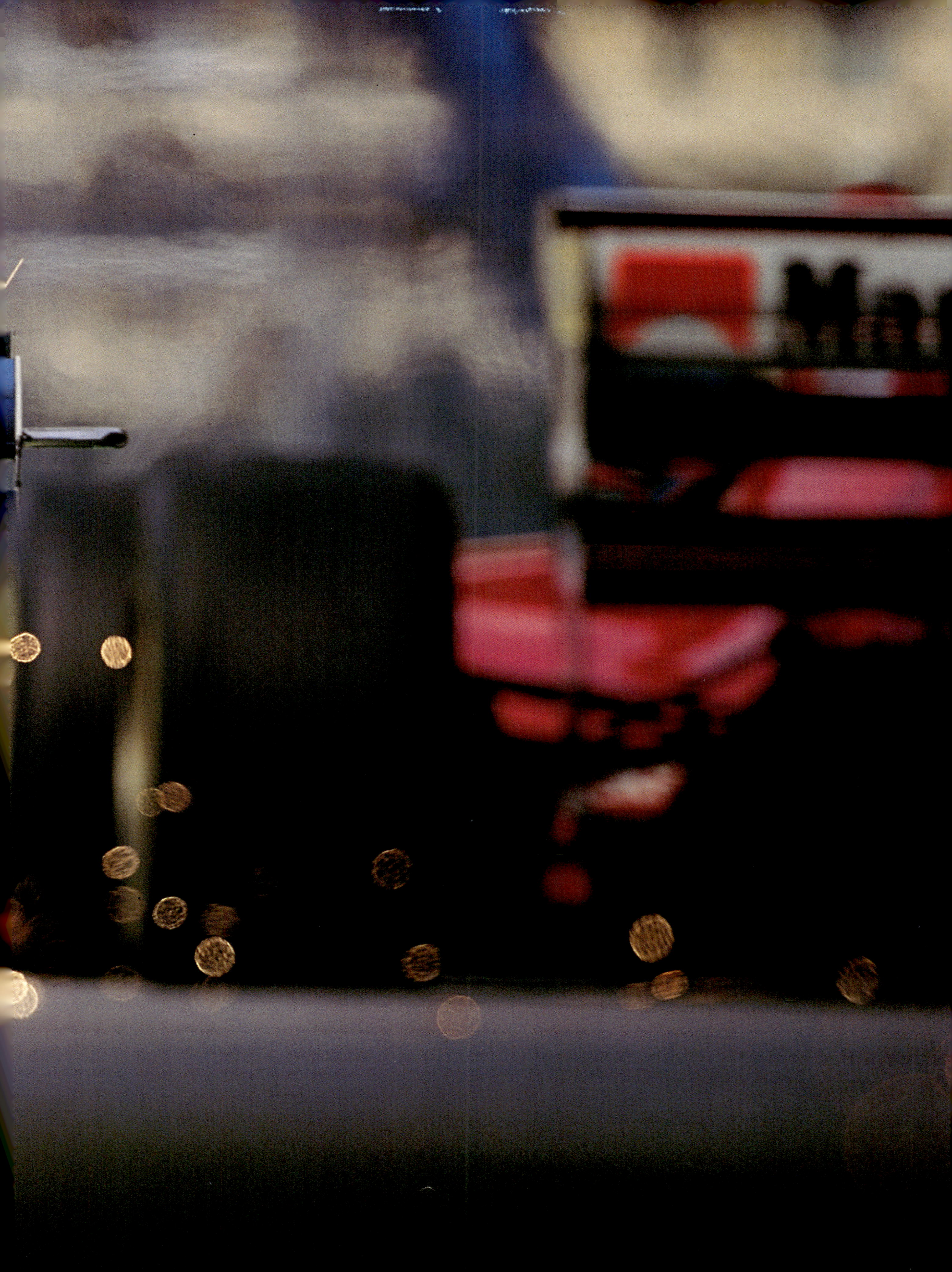

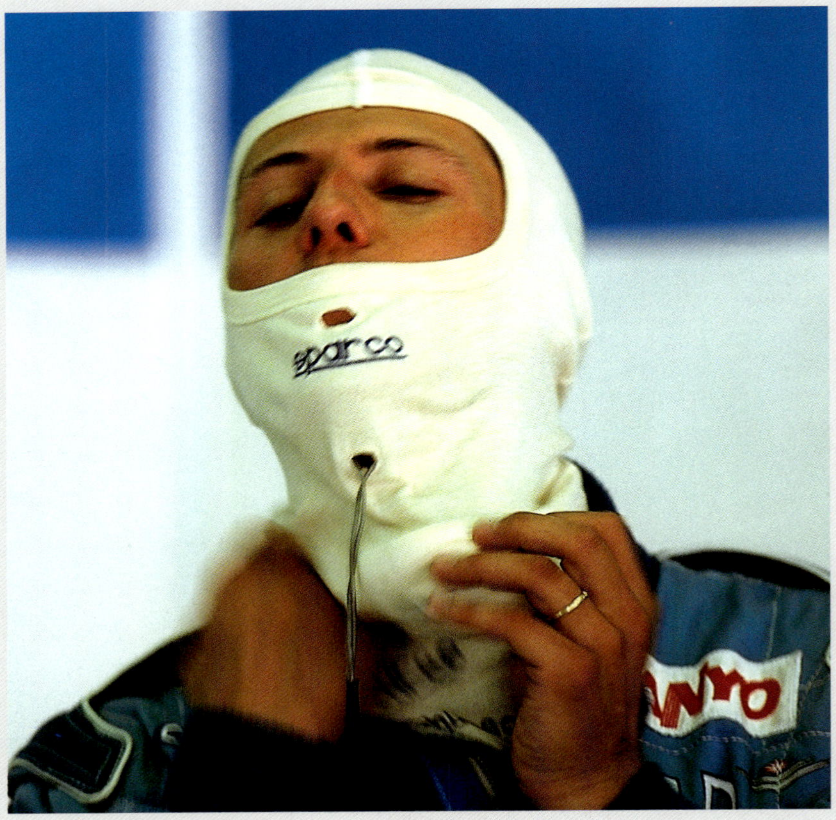

Als Ratzenberger und Senna 1994 in Imola starben, und Karl Wendlinger in Monaco ins Koma fuhr, war die Formel 1 am absoluten Nullpunkt: Michael, Jacky Ickx, Christian Fittipaldi und Berger in Monaco an der Unfallstelle von Wendlinger, vor dem Rennen Trauerminuten für die Toten von Imola. Schumi für zwei Rennen gesperrt, England am grünen Tisch verloren, in Belgien wegen eines reglementwidrigen Unterbodens disqualifiziert, dazu die Unterstellung, Benetton habe in den Tiefen der Software eine verbotene Traktionskontrolle aktiviert: Das alles konnte nicht verhindern, daß Schumi 1994 Weltmeister wurde.

With the death of Ratzenberger and Senna at Imola in 1995, and with Karl Wendlinger falling into a coma after an accident in Monaco, Formula 1 dropped into a deep hole. In Monaco at the place of Wendlinger's accident, Michael, Jacky Ickx, Christian Fittipaldi and Berger observed a moment's silence for those who lost their lives in Imola. Schumi was barred from two races: forfeiting the British Grand Prix through a verdict, and then being disqualified in Belgium when the underbody failed to comply to regulations. Moreover, it was insinuated that Benetton had activated an illegal traction control hidden deep within their software. All this did not prevent Schumi from becoming the 1994 World Champion.

Quando nel 1994 Ratzenberger e Senna muoiono a Imola e Wendlinger a Montecarlo va in coma, la Formula 1 tocca il fondo: Michael, Jackie Ickx, Christian Fittipaldi, Berger a Montecarlo sul punto dell'incidente di Wendlinger; il minuto di silenzio per i morti di Imola prima della gara. Schumi squalificato per due gare, il Gran Premio d'Inghilterra perso a tavolino, in Belgio la squalifica per il fondo irregolare della vettura, e, in piú, l'insinuazione che la Benetton abbia attivato un software per un controllo di trazione non lecito: il tutto non impedisce a Schumi di laurearsi Campione del mondo 1994.

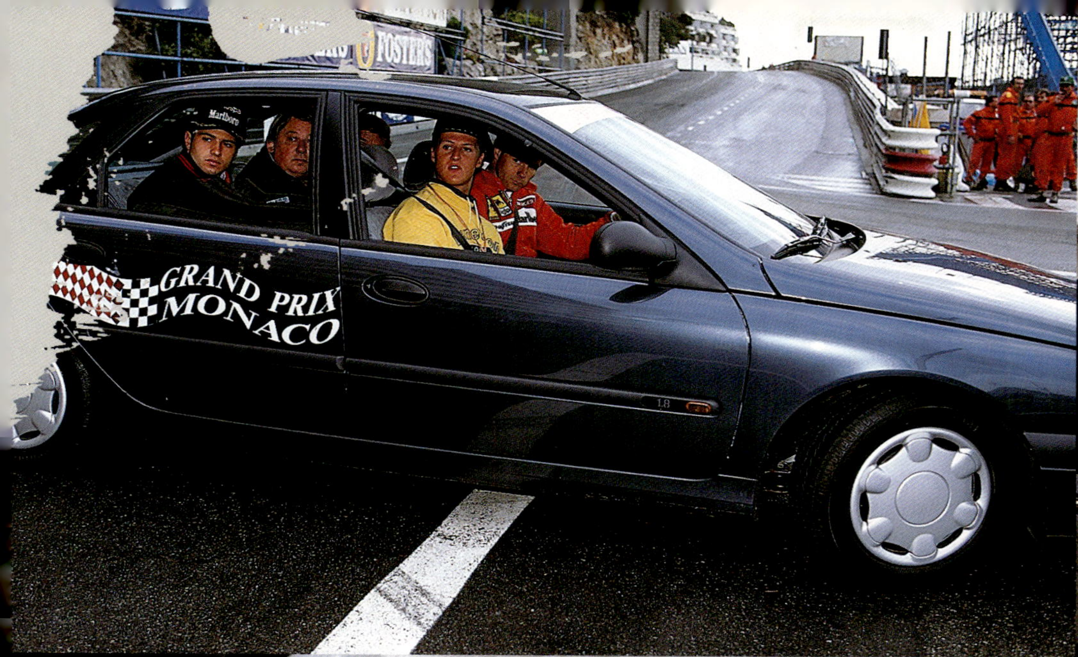
GRAND PRIX
MONACO

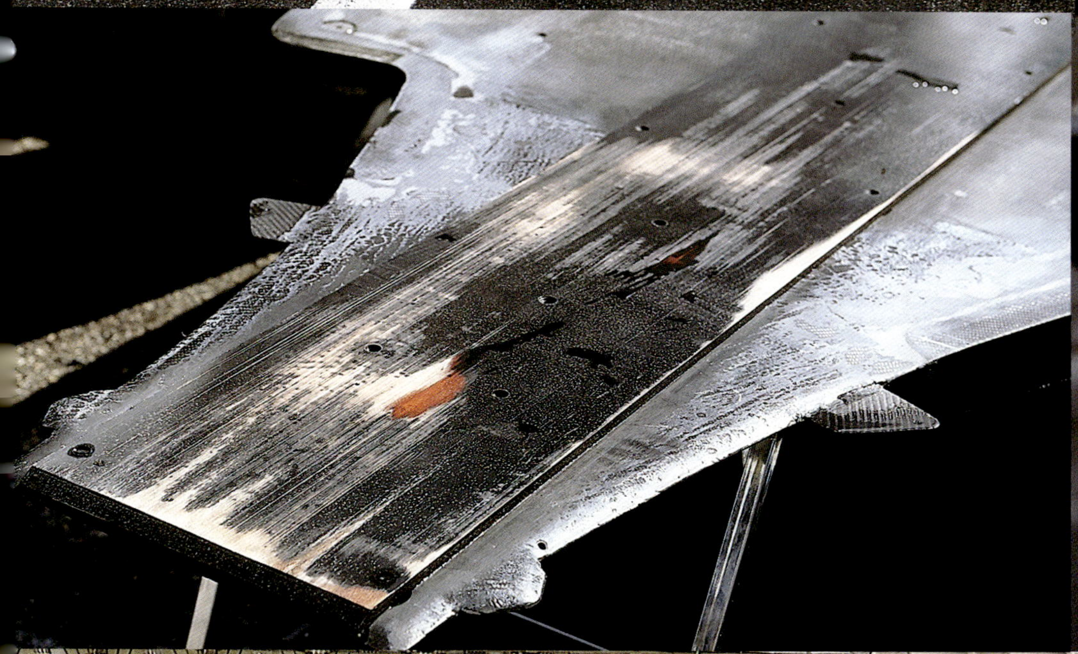

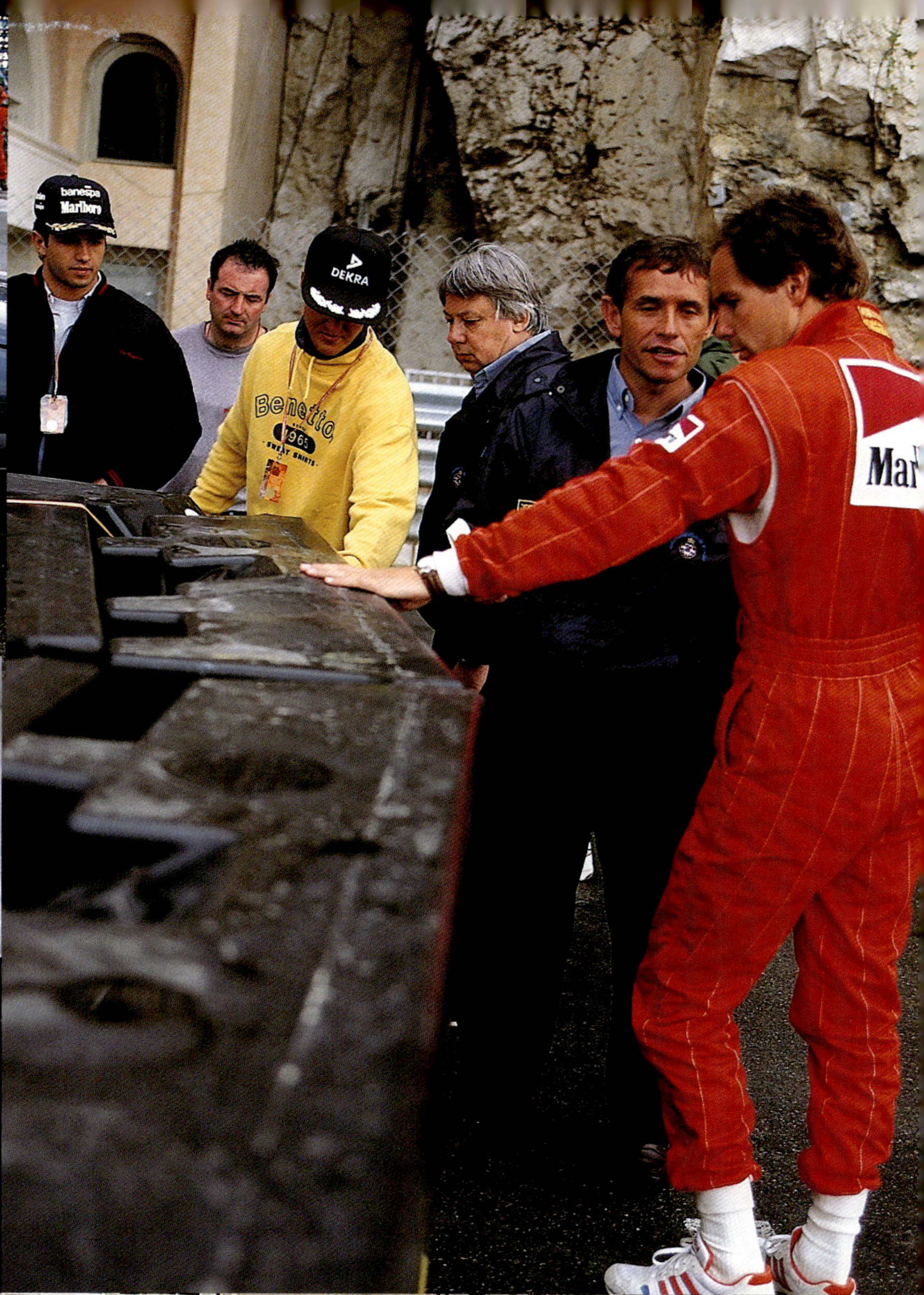

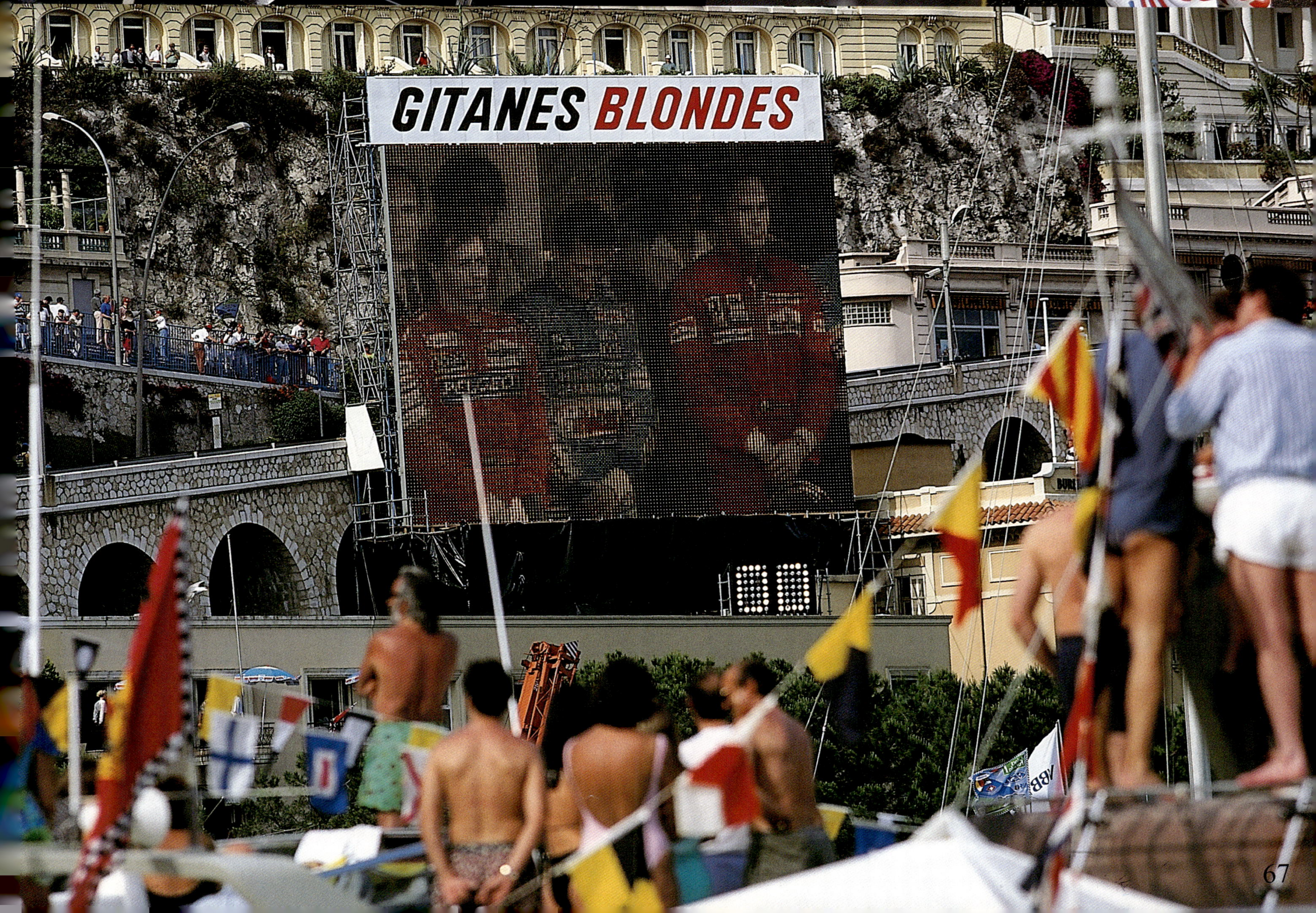
GITANES BLONDES

Die Formel 1 mag als die

Eroberung des Sinnlosen

erscheinen.

Eines ist sie mit Sicherheit:

Das Leben am Limit.

Formula 1 may seem like a

futile conquest.

But it's one thing for sure:

Life at the limit.

La Formula 1 può sembrare

la conquista di ciò che non

ha senso. Sicuramente è...

la vita portata al limite.

69

Je höher er stieg, desto weniger wurden die wahren Freunde. Erfolg treibt einen in die Isolation, seine Hunde werden zu den liebsten Spielgefährten und die Formel 1 immer mehr zu einem Bildschirm-Game der Ingenieure.

The higher he climbed the fewer true friends he had. Success placed him in isolation and his dogs became his favourite playmates. Formula 1 became more and more a monitor-game for engineers.

Piú lui sale in alto, piú diventano rari i veri amici. Il successo lo spinge all'isolamento, i suoi cani sono la compagnia preferita, mentre la Formula 1 si trasforma sempre piú in un video-game degli ingegneri.

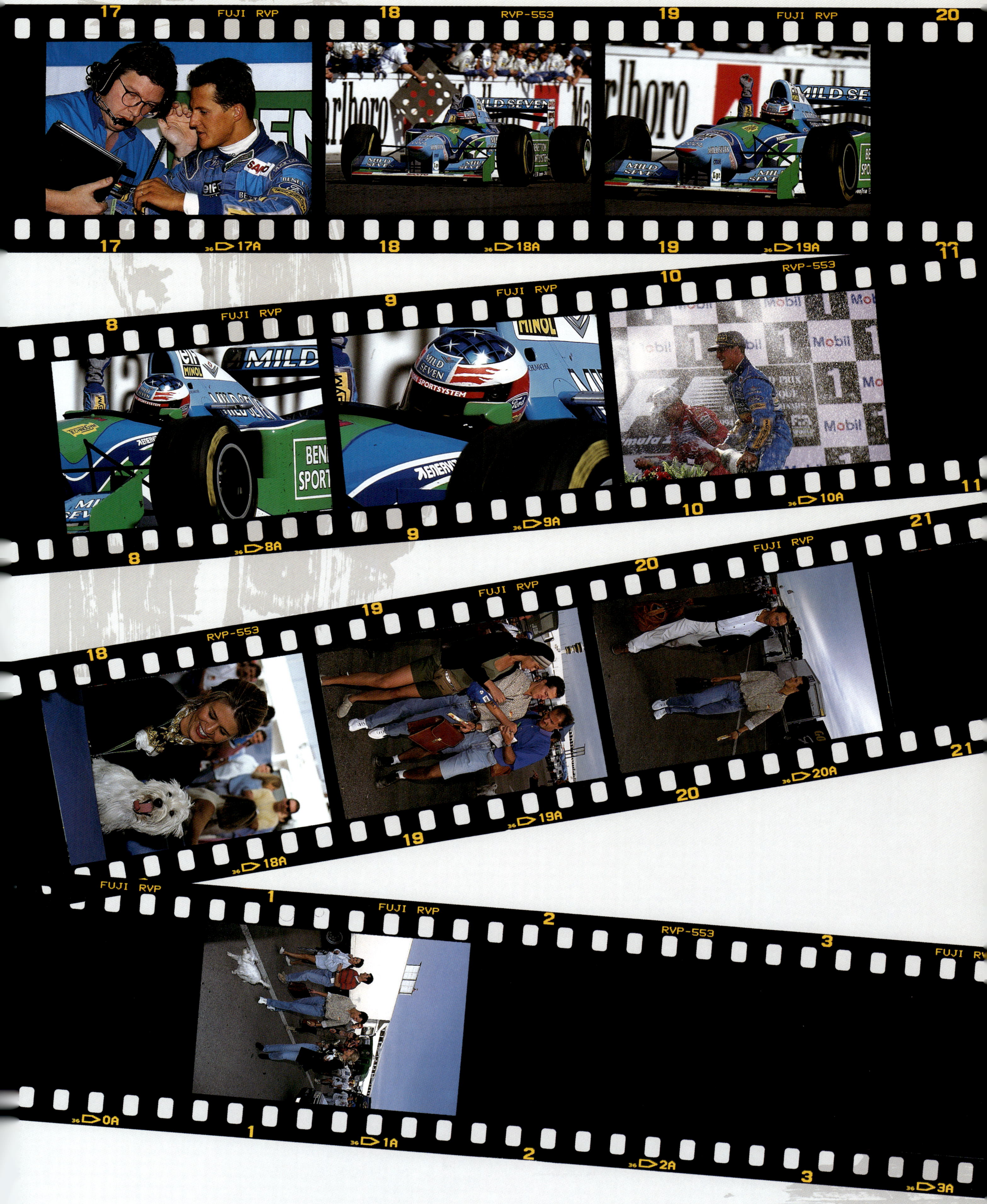

71

72

Die Kollision von Adelaide 1994: Der Benetton benutzte den Hill-Williams als Sprungbrett, stieg in die Luft, landete hart. Michael war sofort Zuschauer, Hill begrub an der Box den Titeltraum. Den Titel widmete Michael „jenem Mann, der unser Bester war, und der nicht mehr unter uns ist - Ayrton Senna."

The Adelaide collision of 1994: The Benetton used Hill's Williams as a launching pad, became airborne, and landed hard. Michael immediately became a spectator, and Hill buried his title dream in the pits. Michael dedicated the title to "a man who was the best and is no longer among us - Ayrton Senna."

La collisione di Adelaide nel 1994: la Williams di Hill fa da trampolino, la Benetton sale, atterra picchiando duro. Michael è subito spettatore, Hill abbandona ai box il sogno iridato. Michael dedica il titolo a colui che era il migliore tra noi e che non è più tra noi: Ayrton Senna.

Willy Weber wurde der Mann hinter Schumi, er spielte die Vater-Mutter-Rolle und wurde sein Schatten. Ohne seine Macher-Qualitäten hätte das Schumacher-Wunder gar nicht stattfinden können. Wenn Michael die Ölquelle ist, so ist Willy Weber, der gelernte Hotelkaufmann aus Regensburg, gewissermaßen der Bohrturm. Ohne Bohrturm wäre das Öl nicht an die Oberfläche gesprudelt. Willy Weber regiert, managt und verwaltet in Stuttgart das Schumacher-Imperium. Die Arbeitsteilung ist perfekt und brillant: Im Cockpit agiert Michael, außerhalb der Willy. Im Verlauf der Jahre entstand eine Zweierseilschaft, die sich beim Gipfelgang auf den Mount Everest des Autorennsport jenseits aller Worte versteht.

Willy Weber became the man behind Schumi. He assumed the role of father and mother, and was his shadow. Without his dynamic qualities the Schumacher-miracle would not have evolved. If Michael was the oil-spring, then Willy Weber, the hotel manager from Regensburg, was the oil-rig so to speak. Without the rig, the oil couldn't be brought to the surface. Willy Weber rules, manages, and administers the Schumacher empire from Stuttgart. The division of labour is perfect and brilliant. Michael reigns in the cockpit, and Willy controls all else. Over the years a strong two-man team developed. On their climb to the peak of motorsport's Mt Everest, their understanding works without words.

Willy Weber è l'uomo dietro Schumi, svolge un ruolo paterno e materno, diventa la sua ombra. Senza le sue doti di pragmatismo il fenomeno-Schumacher non si sarebbe verificato. Se Michael è il pozzo petrolifero, Willy Weber è per cosí dire la… torre di trivellazione. Da Stoccarda, Weber gestisce, sorveglia e amministra l'impero Schumacher. La divisione dei compiti e del lavoro è perfetta e brillante: nel cockpit decide Michael, fuori decide Willy. Nel corso degli anni si forma una cordata a due, che senza perdersi in discorsi sa come portare a buon fine la scalata all'Everest dell'automobilismo sportivo.

75

WE ♥ YOU MICHAE

JEAN!!!
WE'RE GLA
BECAUSE
YOU'RE RI
BRIATORE
Schumi, gib Gas!
Weltmeister 94
Fanclub Leipzig-Gohlis
Corinna
SCHUMI
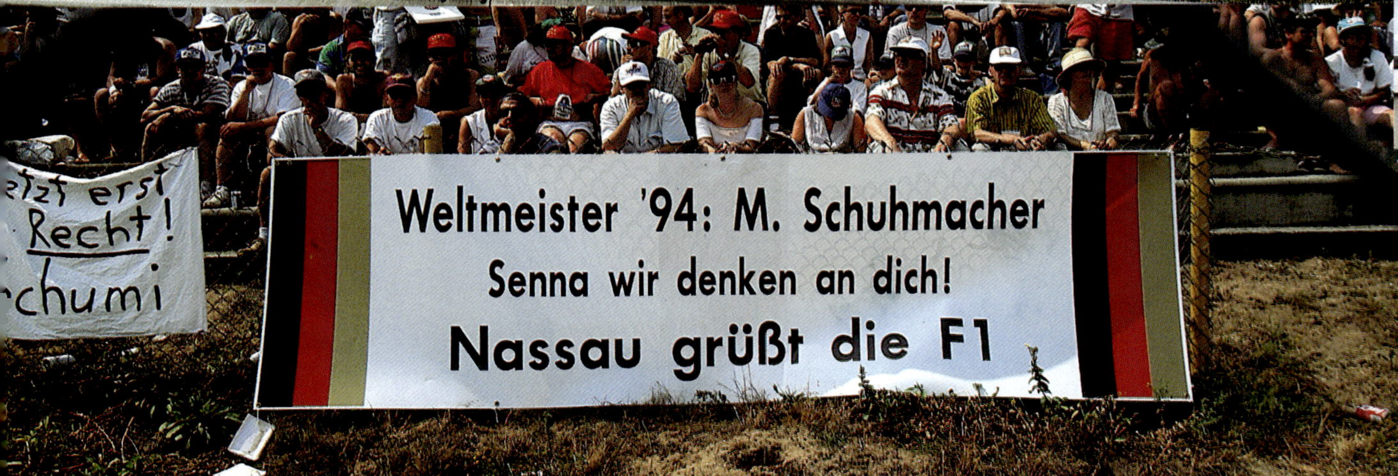
Weltmeister '94: M. Schuhmacher
Senna wir denken an dich!
Nassau grüßt die F1
Recht!

Windflöte
grüßt
M. Schumacher
WORMS GRÜSST
MICHAEL SCHUMACHER

MILD SEVEN
5
M. SCHUMACHER
F1-CHAMPION
BENETTON

SCHUMAC
WER SONS
M. Schumacher

Es kann
nur
geben
Michael
Schumacher
Fan Club

KERPEN grüsst
MICHAEL SCHUMACHER

BAD WIESSEE
GRÜSST
SCHUMACHER

MI CHAEL

Forza
Michael

右京
がんばれ!

GERMAN
grüßt

Joschi und Kreuzle
grüßen
unseren sau schnellen
Michael Schumacher

grüßt
Duisburg

BAMBINIS
grüßen
GOODYEAR
GOODYEAR

M.Schumacher

Jenny Halfon, eine führende britische Graphologin analysiert Schumis dreizeilige englische Schriftprobe zu folgendem Psychogramm:

Er vertraut seinem Instinkt. Klarer Verstand, weiß, was er will. Mehr durch Kraft gelenkt als durch Urteilsvermögen. Er denkt in Gesamtkonzepten und nicht in systematischen Abläufen. Er ist phantasiereich. Er beurteilt alles für sich. Wenn er den letzten Umkehrpunkt überschreitet, kann er wie ein Vulkan ausbrechen, denn er ist von Natur aus feurig. Er ist leicht zu beleidigen und empfindlich verletzbar. Er lacht und weint leicht. Es gibt keine Halbheiten. Er liebt einerseits die Verwirrung, andererseits haßt er das Vergiften. Er ist seine eigene Triebfeder und versucht sich ständig zu verbessern, um Schwachpunkte in Stärke umzudrehen. Er will alles nach seinem Zeitplan erledigen. Er ist extrem pünktlich und präzise. Sein Herz bestimmt den Verstand, was persönliche, vertraute Beziehungen betrifft. Er hat eine exzellente Beurteilung, was Zeit, Distanz und Raum betrifft. Sein Selbstvertrauen kommt aus dem Inneren. Willy Weber: „Diese Punkte werde ich voll unterschreiben...."

Jenny Halfon, a leading British graphologist, analysed three lines of Schumi's handwriting in English and came up with the following profile:

He trusts his instincts. Clear reasoning ability - he knows what he wants. Directed more by power than by faculty of judgement. He thinks in overall concepts rather than systematic sequences. He's highly imaginative. He makes his own opinions. When he's pushed beyond the final turning point he can erupt like a volcano - by nature he's fiery. He is easily offended and vulnerable. He laughs and cries easily. There are no half measures. On the one hand he loves chaos, but hates intrigue. He motivates himself, constantly trying to better himself, turning his weak points around to become strong points. He wants to achieve everything within his timeplan. He is extremely punctual and precise. His heart rules his head when it comes to personal, trusting relationships. He has excellent judgement concerning time, space and distance. His self-esteem comes from within. Willy Weber: "I fully endorse this point."

Jenny Halfon, nota grafologa inglese analizza un campione calligrafico di tre righe di Schumi e ne traccia il seguente psicogramma:

Si fida del proprio intuito, pensa logicamente, sa quel che vuole. Si lascia guidare più dalla propria forza che dal raziocinio. Ragiona in termini complessivi e non per processi sistematici. Ha una fervida immaginazione. Valuta tutto in riferimento a se stesso. Se oltrepassa il punto di non ritorno può diventare un vulcano, perché per natura è irruente. È molto sensibile e leggermente permaloso. Ride e piange facilmente. Per lui non esistono mezzi termini. Da un lato ama la confusione, dall'altro odia gli intrighi. È la molla di se stesso e cerca di migliorarsi continuamente per trasformare i punti deboli in punti di forza. Vuol fare tutto secondo i propri ritmi. È estremamente puntuale, puntiglioso e preciso. Nei rapporti interpersonali e familiari il cuore ha il sopravvento sulla ragione. Ha uno spiccato senso del tempo, della distanza e dello spazio. La fiducia in se stesso emana da dentro.
Willy Weber: "Potrei confermare e sottoscrivere immediatamente quanto sopra…"

Corinna ist die Frau an seiner Seite.
Sport und Bewegung ist sein Leben.

Corinna is the woman at his side.
Sport and movement are his life.

Corinna è la donna al suo fianco.
Lo sport e il movimento sono la sua vita.

DEKRA
MILD SEVEN

DEKRA
FORMULA 1 WORLD CHAMPION 1994
MILD SEVEN

3 bis 4 g an Querbeschleunigung ist er aus der Formel 1 gewöhnt. Als Co-Pilot im Mach 2 schnellen Bundeswehr-Tornado mußte er die obligate Anti-g-Hose tragen, die durch Zusammenpressen der unteren Extremitäten bei hohen g-Belastungen das Gehirn vor Blutleere bewahrt.

A Formula 1 pilot is accustomed to 3 to 4g acceleration. As co-pilot in a Mach 2 Airforce Tornado he was obliged to wear Anti-g-trousers, which by compressing the body's lower extremities at times of high g-forces, protect the brain from lack of blood.

In F1 è abituato a 3-4 g di accelerazione trasversale. Come copilota sul Tornado Mach 2 dell'aeronautica militare deve indossare obbligatoriamente la tuta anti-g, che mediante una compressione degli arti inferiori in presenza di elevati valori g evita il deflusso di sangue dal cervello.

45+73

Jesus Christ Superstar?
Die Hände, die nach Berührung
lechzen, würden darauf
hindeuten...

Jesus Christ Superstar?
The groping hands reaching out
to touch make you think..

Jesus Christ Superstar?
Le mani protese sembrerebbero
dire di sì...

85

In Hockenheim 1995 sagte Benetton-Boss Flavio Briatore: „Schumi schneidert sich mit seinen Technikern einen Maßanzug, der niemand anderem paßt... wir sind eine richtige Familie..." Und trotzdem stand Michael mit einem Fuß schon bei Ferrari, was Briatore zu dem Ausspruch veranlaßte: „Wenn ich ihn verliere, geb' ich mir die Kugel..." Schumi gewann Hockenheim, unterschrieb in einem Hotel in Monaco den Ferrari-Vertrag, Flavio lebt immer noch...

In Hockenheim 1995 Benetton boss Flavio Briatore remarked: "Schumi and his technicians created a tailor-made suit for him which fits nobody else...we're a really close family." Nevertheless, Michael already had one foot in the door at Ferrari which gave Briatore reason to remark: "If I lose him, I'll shoot myself!" Schumi won Hockenheim, signed the Ferrari contract in a Monaco hotel room. Flavio still lives ...

Flavio Briatore a Hockenheim nel '95: "Insieme ai suoi tecnici Schumi sta mettendo a punto un vestito su misura che non va bene a nessun altro... siamo una vera famiglia..." Ciò nonostante Michael ha già un piede in casa Ferrari, il che fa dire a Briatore: "Se lo perdo mi sparo..."
Schumi vince a Hockenheim, in un albergo di Montecarlo sottoscrive il contratto con la Ferrari, Flavio è vivo e vegeto...

GROSSER MOBIL 1 PREIS VON DEUTSCHLAND HOCKENHEIM 1995

Die Choreographie des Benetton-Balletts beim Boxenstopp war deshalb so perfekt, weil tagtäglich trainiert wurde.

1. Sekunde: Preßluftschrauber
              lösen Radmuttern,
              Wagenheber in Aktion,
              Tankschlauch eingeklinkt
2. Sekunde: Radwechsel
3. Sekunde: Neue Räder
4. Sekunde: Runter vom Wagenheber
5. Sekunde: Go

The choreography of the Benetton ballet troupe in the pits was perfect...., they trained every day.

1st second: nut-gun loosens the wheel nut,
car jack in action, connect refueling hose
2nd second: wheel change
3rd second: new wheels
4th second: release car jack
5th second: Go

Grazie a un allenamento quotidiano, la coreografia del balletto Benetton alla sosta ai box raggiunge praticamente la perfezione:

1° secondo: svitamento dadi ruote, sollevamento vettura, inserimento tubo rifornimento
2° secondo: smontaggio ruote
3° secondo: montaggio ruote
4° secondo: abbassamento vettura
5° secondo: Go!

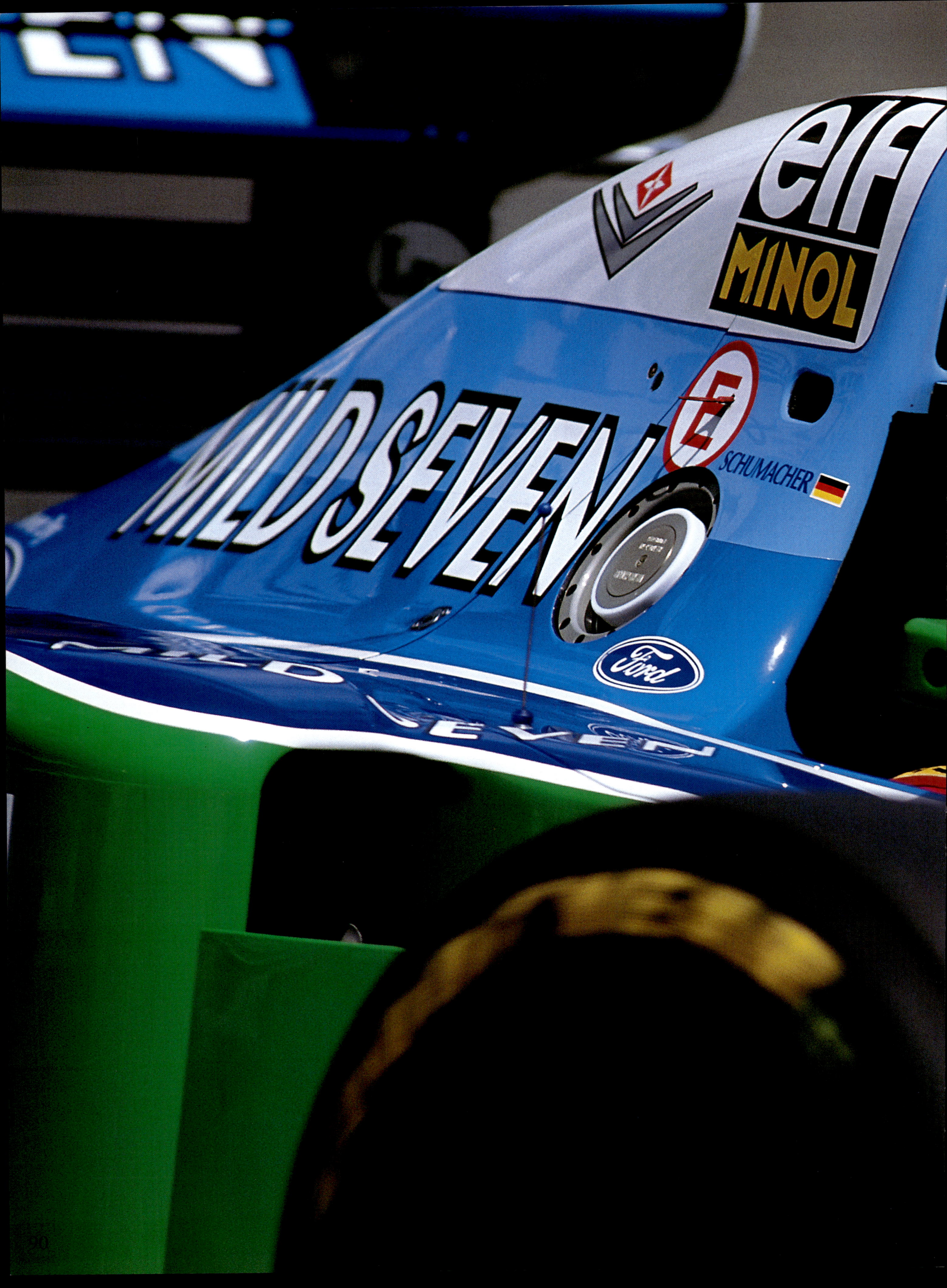
elf
MINOL
MILD SEVEN
SCHUMACHER
Ford

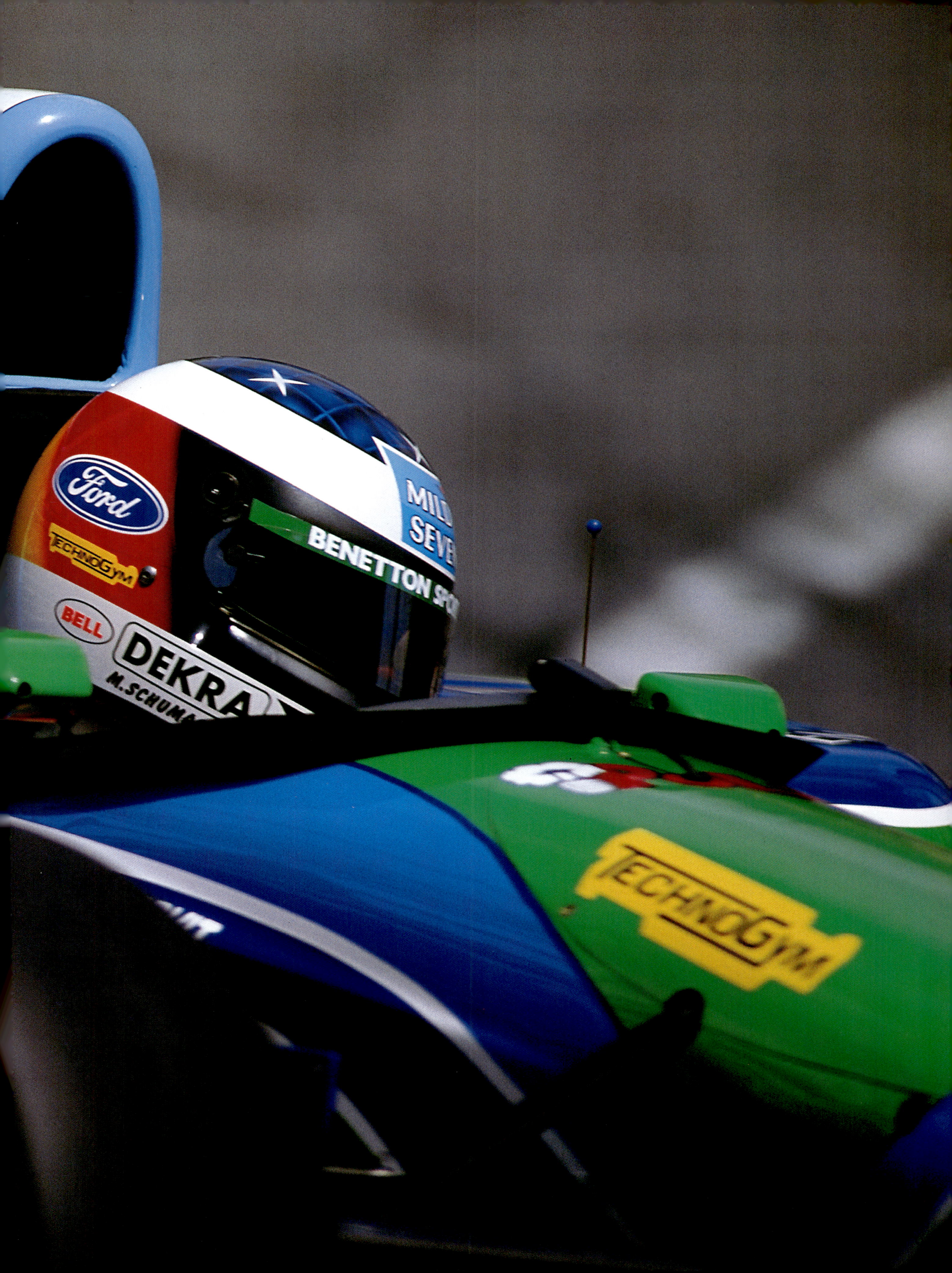

Ford
TECHNOGYM
BELL
DEKRA
TECHNOGYM

ALS DAMON HILL DEN SCHUMI NICHT MEHR BESIEGEN KONNTE, LIESS ER SICH ZU DEM AUSSPRUCH HINREISSEN, ER HABE ES MIT EINEM „GEKLONTEN" GEGNER ZU TUN. EINEN GIFTIGEREN PFEIL KONNTE HILL NICHT MEHR ABSCHIESSEN. DEUTLICHER FREILICH KONNTE ER SEINE OHNMACHT NICHT MEHR DARSTELLEN.

WHEN DAMON HILL COULD NO LONGER BEAT SCHUMI, HE LET SLIP THAT HIS OPPONENT WAS A RESULT OF CLONING. HE COULDN'T HAVE SHOT A MORE POISONOUS ARROW. AT THE SAME TIME, HE COULDN'T HAVE STATED HIS FEELING OF POWERLESSNESS MORE CLEARLY.

NEL MOMENTO IN CUI NON RIESCE PIÚ A BATTERE SCHUMI, DAMON HILL DICHIARA DI AVER A CHE FARE UN AVVERSARIO "CLONATO". NON AVREBBE POTUTO SCOCCARE FRECCIATA PIÚ VELENOSA, E AL TEMPO STESSO NON AVREBBE POTUTO MANIFESTARE IN MANIERA PIÚ ELOQUENTE LA PROPRIA IMPOTENZA.

MILD SEVEN
RENAULT
elf
MILD SEVEN
MILD SEVEN
BENETTON SPORTSYSTEM
MILD SEVEN
1

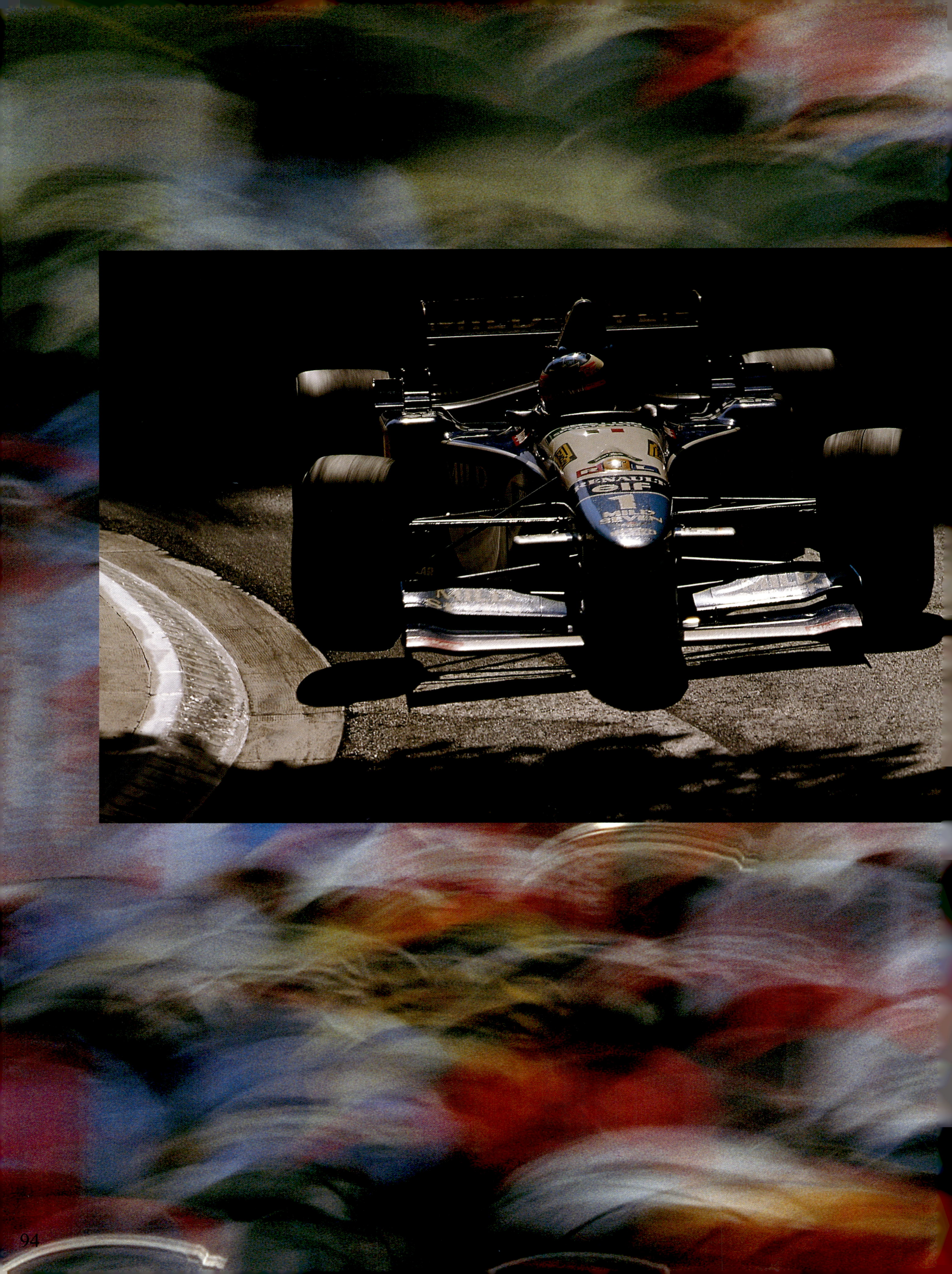
RENAULT
elf
1
MILD SEVEN

Monaco wurde eine Zwischenstation seines Lebens. Nicht nur, weil sich das Fürstentum als Steueroase anbot, sondern auch als Tauchstation für ein ruhigeres Leben.

Monaco was a crossroad in his life. Not only because of the Principality's tax-haven status, but also because it was a tranquil oasis.

Il Principato di Monaco diventa una tappa fondamentale nella vita di Michael, non solo come paradiso fiscale, ma anche come rifugio nel quale vivere un po' di tranquillità.

Er hat die Simultan-Kapazität eines Jumbo-Kaptns. Nich
Renndistanz am Limit zu fahren, Senna nannte es „ein gew
einen Funkverkehr mit der Box zu führen, um sich über Ge
Auto hineinzuhorchen.

He has the simultaneous capacity of a jumbo captain: Hi
racing distance at the limit. (Senna called it, "to mentally
contact with the pits, to inform himself about opponents
car.

Schumi possiede le capacità simultanee di un pilota di ju
limite per una gara intera (Senna diceva: "tenere menta
contatto radio con i box per ricevere informazioni sugli
nuamente la propria vettura.

nur, daß ihm seine ungeheure Fitneß erlaubt, eine volle
sses Tempo geistig durchzuhalten", er ist auch noch fähig,
ner und Strategien zu informieren und gleichzeitig in sein

unbelievable fitness not only enables him to drive a full
maintain a certain tempo.") He is also able to stay in radio
d strategies, while at the same time tuning in to his own

bo. Grazie all'eccellente forma fisica riesce a guidare al
ente una determinata velocità") mantenendo un costante
versari e le strategie e al tempo stesso "ascoltare" conti-

DEKRA
MILD SEVEN
TECHNOGYM
MILD SEVEN
Kickers
Bitburger
BENETTON SPORT SYSTEM
M. Schumacher
sparco
Benetton Formula 1
USAG
CHAMPION
devil

Kein Sieger ist so frisch wie er. Mit der Kraft der Jugend wischt er alle Strapazen weg. Austrainiert und willensstark und voller Selbstdisziplin treibt er mit seiner Coolness die Gegner vor, im und nach dem Rennen auf die billigen Stehplätze...

No winner is as fresh as Schumi. With his youthful energy he blasts away all stresses and strains. Highly trained and powered up, strong-willed and self-disciplined - he level-headedly propels himself ahead of his rivals, relegating them to the cheap seats.

Nessun vincitore al traguardo mostra la sua freschezza. Con l'energia della giovane età spazza via i segni della fatica. Perfettamente allenato, dotato di una grandissima forza di volontà e autodisciplina, con la sua freddezza mette in fila gli avvversari prima, durante e dopo la gara...

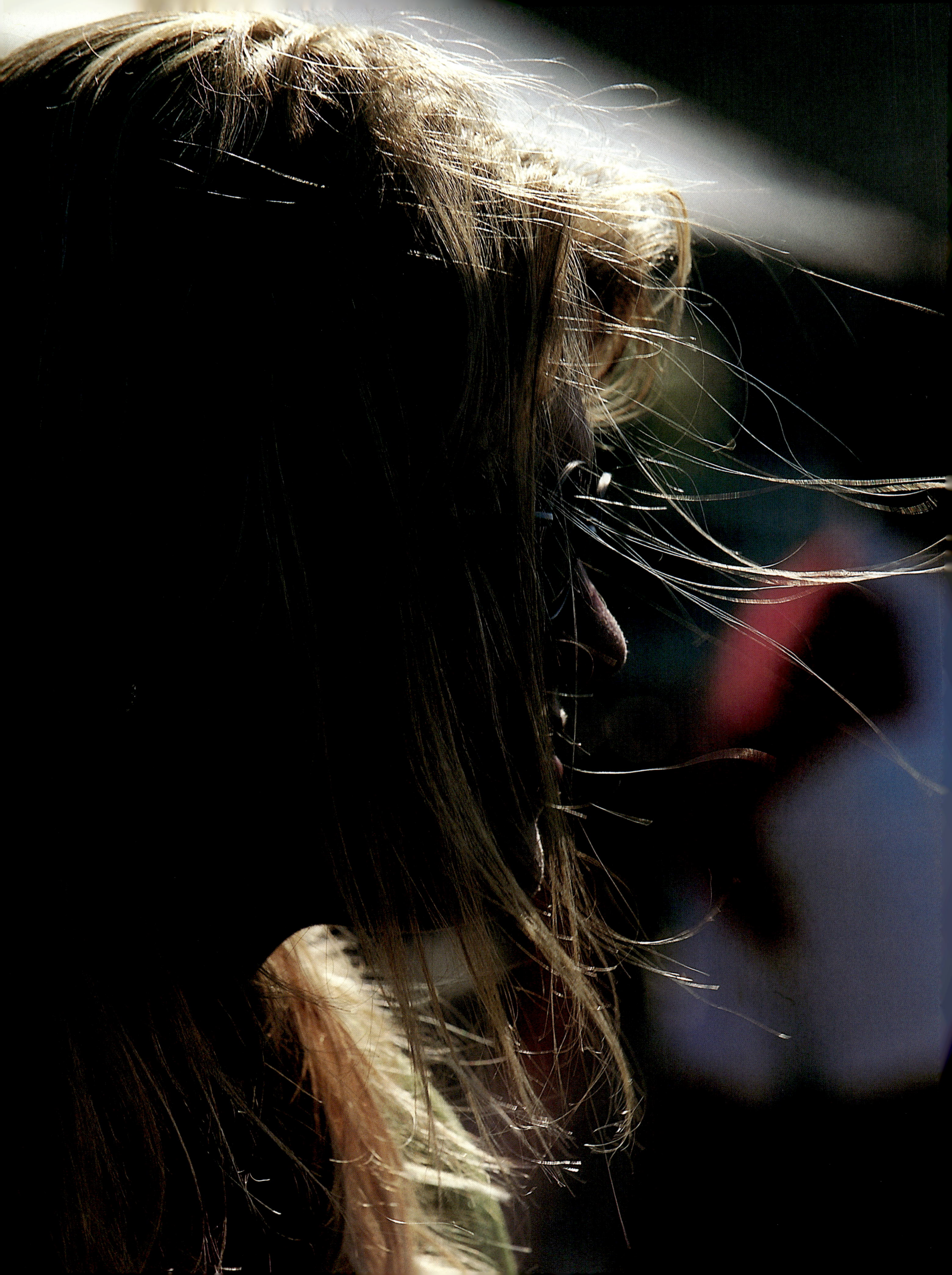

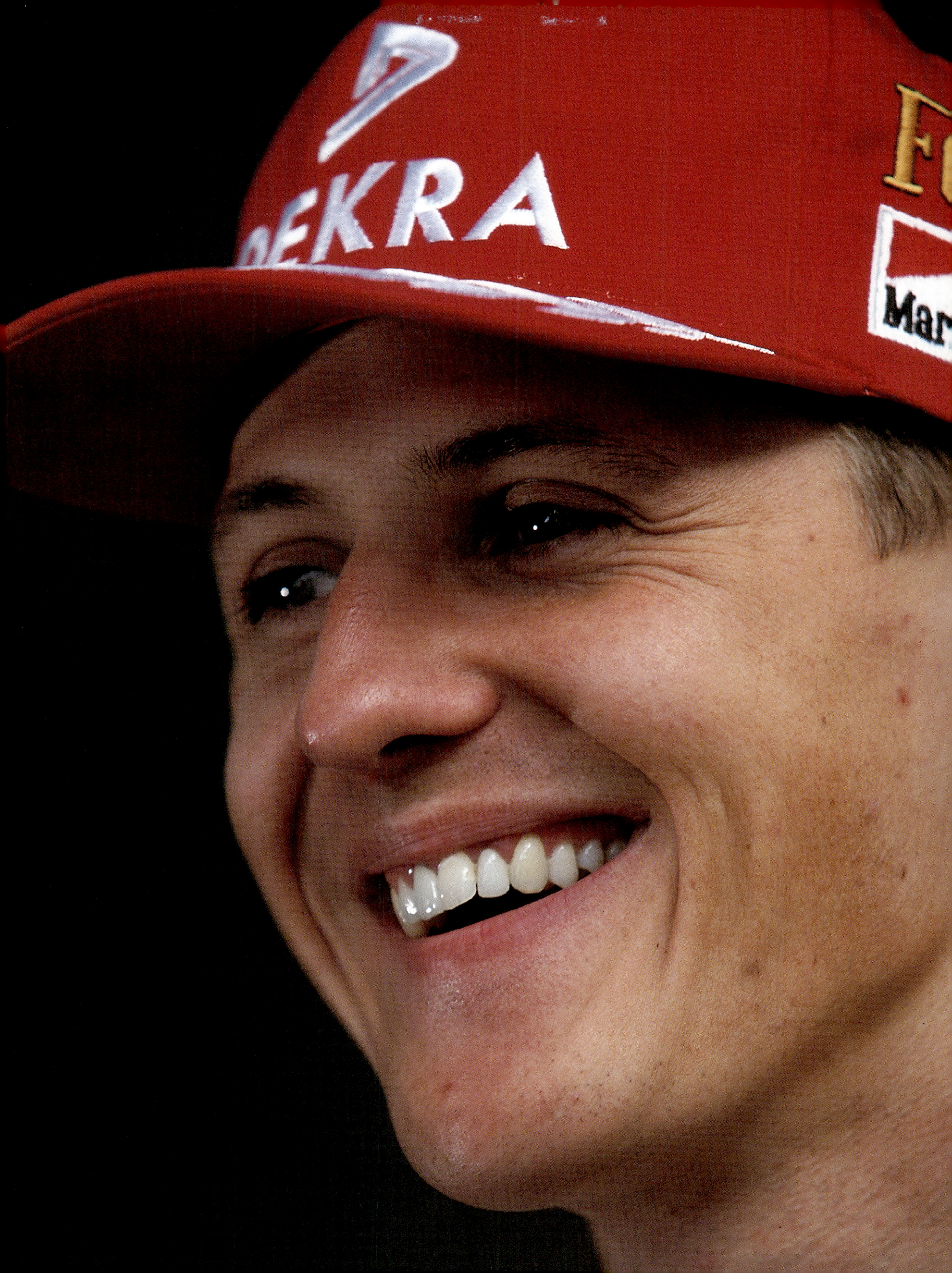
EKRA

Niki Lauda-Jean Todt - Luca di Montezemolo - Agnelli: Das war für Schumacher - Weber im Jahre 1995 die Gesprächs-Stafette zu Ferrari. „Geld hatte nicht die Priorität", versichert Willy Weber, „Michael ist ein Siegertyp und will gewinnen. Das krönende Endziel muß immer der WM-Titel sein." Mit Schumi brach Ferrari zu neuen Ufern auf und Präsident Montezemolo empfing ihn mit offenen Armen, wissend: Wenn wir mit Michael nicht Weltmeister werden, dann liegt es nur an uns...

Niki Lauda - Jean Todt - Luca di Montezemolo – and then Giovanni Agnelli: That was the negotiation gauntlet that Schumacher and Weber ran in 1995 to reach the Ferrari cockpit. "Money wasn't the priority," assures Willy Weber, "Michael is a winning type, and he wants to win. The crowning glory is always the world championship title." With Schumi, Ferrari set out for new shores and President Montezemolo welcomed him with open arms, but also with the knowledge: When we can't become world champion with Michael, then it's our own fault...

Niki Lauda - Jean Todt - Luca di Montezemolo - Agnelli: è questa la sequenza dei colloqui per Schumacher-Weber nel 1995. "La cosa che contava di più non erano i soldi", assicura Willy Weber, "Michael è un vincitore e come tale ha un solo obiettivo: vincere. La mèta e il coronamento di tutto resta sempre e comunque il titolo mondiale." Con Schumi, per la Ferrari si apre una nuova stagione e il presidente Montezemolo lo accoglie a braccia aperte ben sapendo che: Se non vinciamo il mondiale con Schumacher è soltanto colpa nostra...

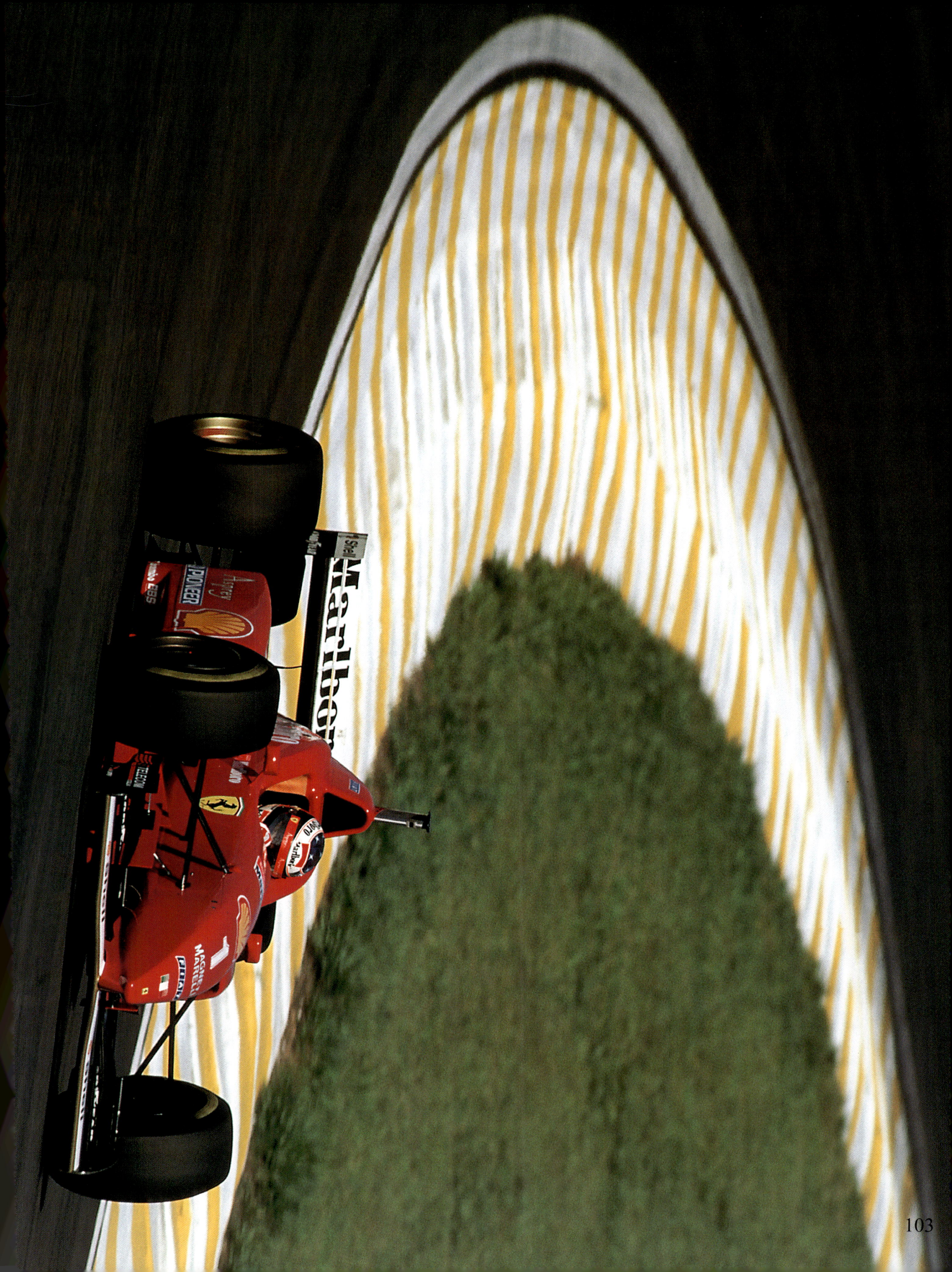
Shell
PIONEER
TELECOM

DER MYTHOS, DER WIE EIN EWIGES LICHT BRENNT „UND VON DER PERSON ENZO FERRARI AUSGING" (NIKI LAUDA), WAR FÜR SCHUMI EIN FREMDWORT, DENN ALS ENZO FERRARI IM AUGUST 1988 STARB, FUHR ER NOCH IN DER FORMEL KÖNIG... SEHR SCHNELL WURDE ER IM FERRARI-TEAM DIE SCHLÜSSELFIGUR, SO WIE ER IN DER FORMEL-1-RIEGE ZUM BESTEN UND BESTVERDIENENDEN PILOTEN AVANCIERT WAR.

THE FERRARI MYTH, BURNING LIKE AN ETERNAL FLAME, "WHICH WAS FOUNDED ON THE MAN ENZO FERRARI" (NIKI LAUDA), WAS FOREIGN TO SCHUMI. WHEN ENZO FERRARI DIED IN AUGUST 1988, MICHAEL WAS STILL COMPETING IN FORMULA KÖNIG... HE VERY QUICKLY BECAME THE KEY FIGURE IN THE FERRARI TEAM, IN EXACTLY THE SAME WAY THAT HE BECAME THE BEST AND HIGHEST PAID PILOT IN THE FORMULA 1 SQUAD.

IL MITO ETERNO "LEGATO AL PERSONAGGIO DI ENZO FERRARI" (NIKI LAUDA) PER SCHUMI È SCONOSCIUTO, POICHÉ QUANDO NEL 1988 IL COMMENDATORE MUORE LUI CORRE ANCORA NELLA FORMULA KÖNIG... MA RAPIDAMENTE MICHAEL DIVENTA LA FIGURA-CHIAVE DELLA SQUADRA FERRARI E IL PILOTA MIGLIORE E PIÚ PAGATO DELLA FORMULA UNO.

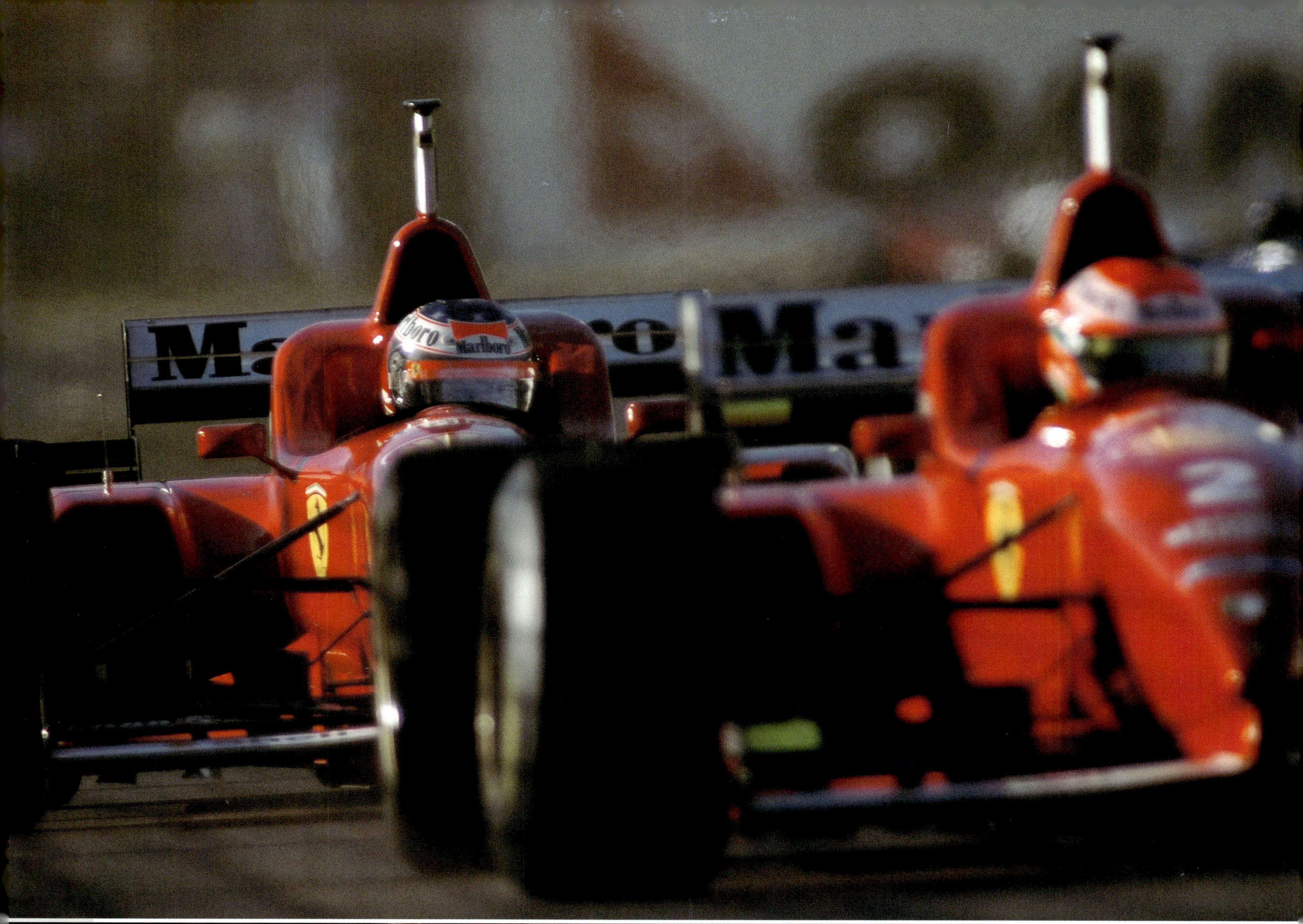

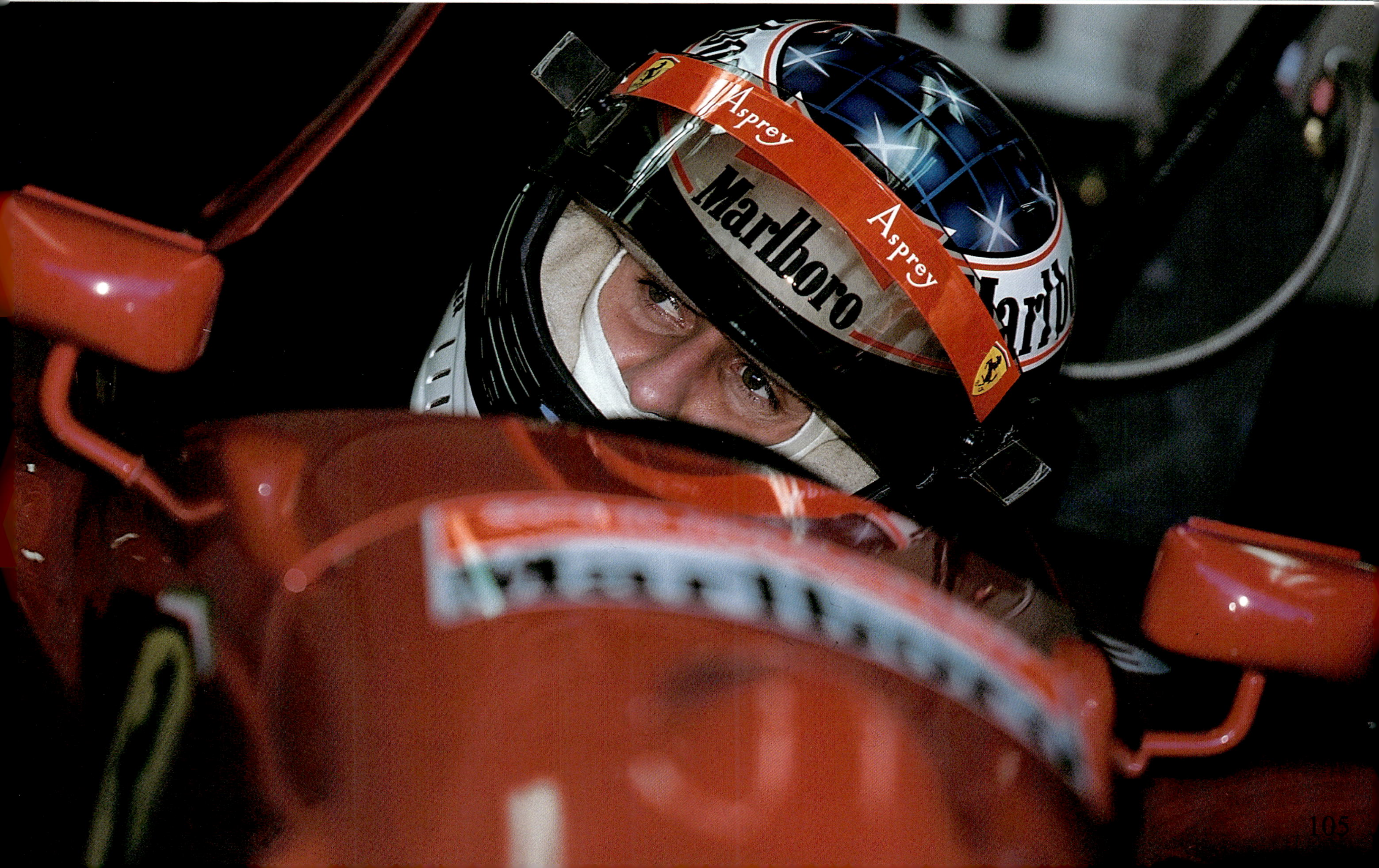
Asprey
Marlboro
Asprey

Ob ausbrechendes Heck, ob Untersteuerer, dank seiner Reflexe wird er auch mit kritischen Autos fertig, wie der Benetton eines war und der Ferrari in seiner ersten Saison 1996 eines ist.

Whether oversteer or understeer, thanks to his reflexes he can master difficult cars - the likes of the Benetton, and the Ferrari during his first season in 1996.

Sia in caso di scodata che di sottosterzo, grazie ai riflessi eccezionali riesce a dominare anche vetture dal comportamento critico, come in passato la Benetton e la Ferrari alla sua prima stagione nel 1996.

750 PS von Ferrari – und die Kupplung von Sachs.

mannesmann automotive Sachs

Motordrehzahl 16.500 min^{-1} - Kupplungstemperatur 1.250° C.

Beim Start eines Formel 1 Boliden werden Kräfte frei, die jedes Vorstellungsvermögen sprengen - und manchmal auch das Material. Spitzenteams wie Ferrari verlassen sich deshalb auf die Funktionssicherheit einer SACHS Rennsportkupplung. Schließlich ist ein gelungener Start noch immer die beste Voraussetzung für ein gutes Ergebnis.

SACHS
KUPPLUNGEN UND STOSSDÄMPFER

Official Supplier to Scuderia Ferrari

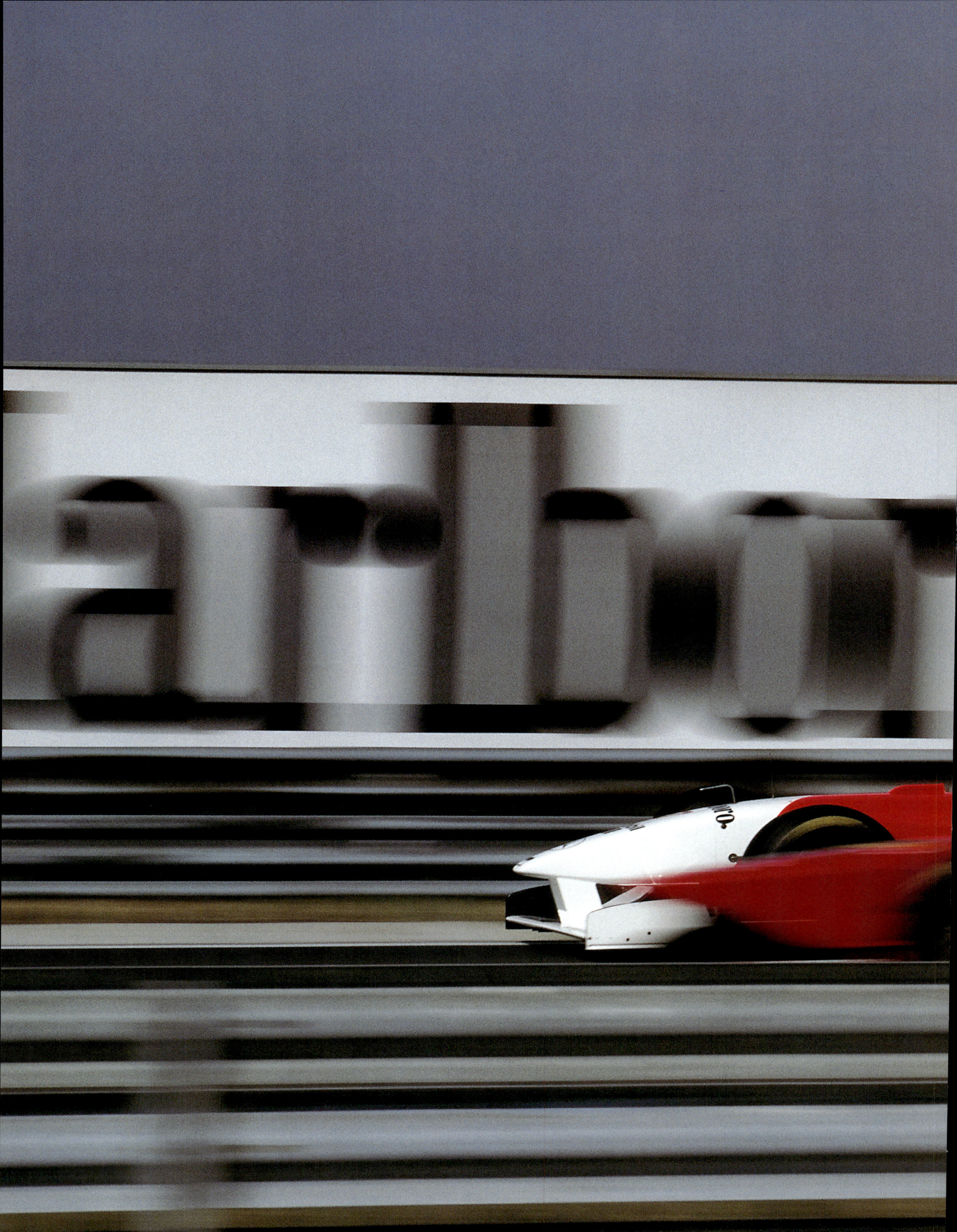

750 PS von Ferrari – und die Kupplung von Sachs.

Motordrehzahl 16.500 min⁻¹ - Kupplungstemperatur 1.250° C.

Beim Start eines Formel 1 Boliden werden Kräfte frei, die jedes Vorstellungsvermögen sprengen - und manchmal auch das Material. Spitzenteams wie Ferrari verlassen sich deshalb auf die Funktionssicherheit einer SACHS Rennsportkupplung. Schließlich ist ein gelungener Start noch immer die beste Voraussetzung für ein gutes Ergebnis.

mannesmann Sachs automotive

SACHS
KUPPLUNGEN UND STOSSDÄMPFER

Official Supplier to Scuderia Ferrari

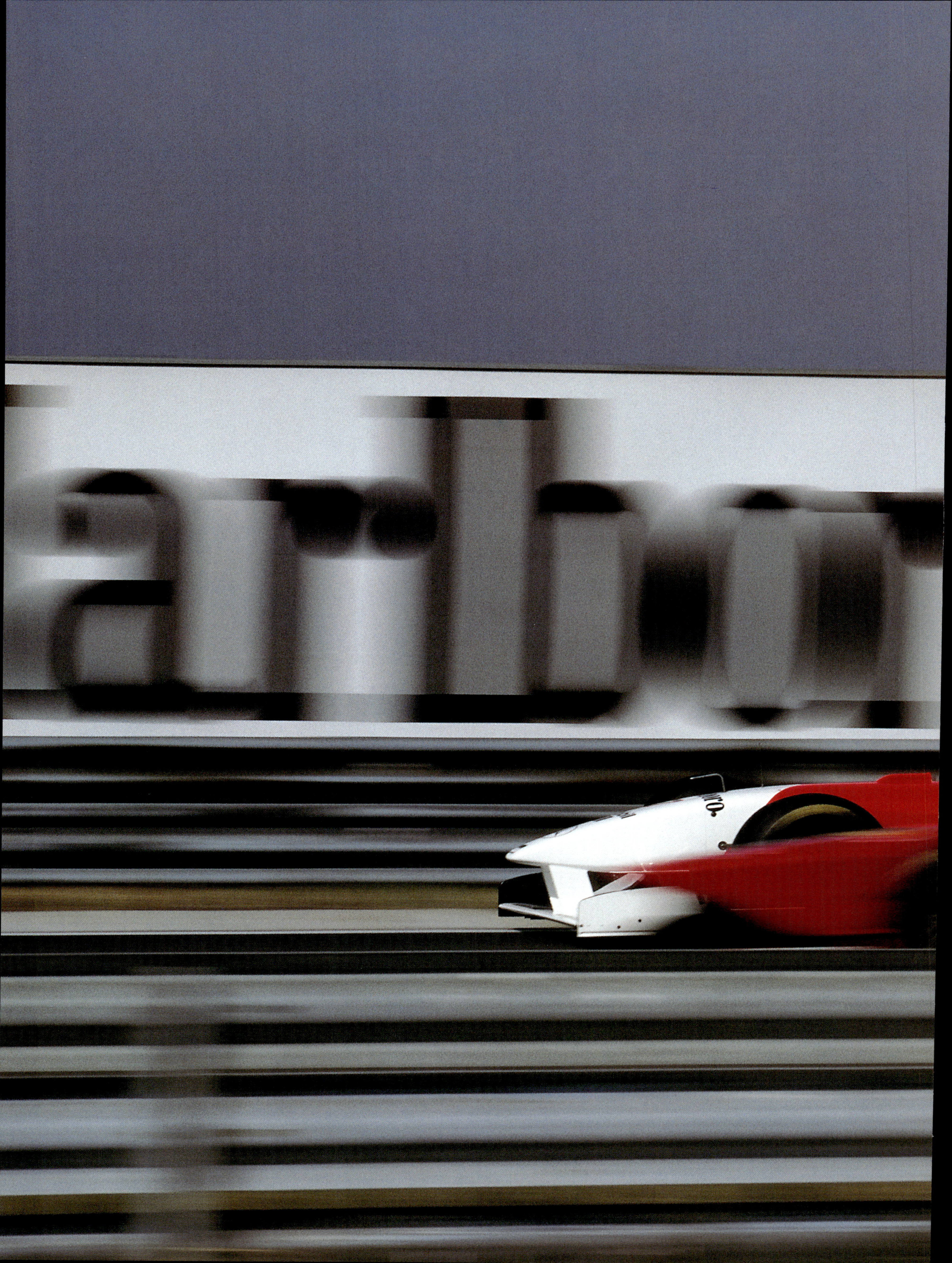

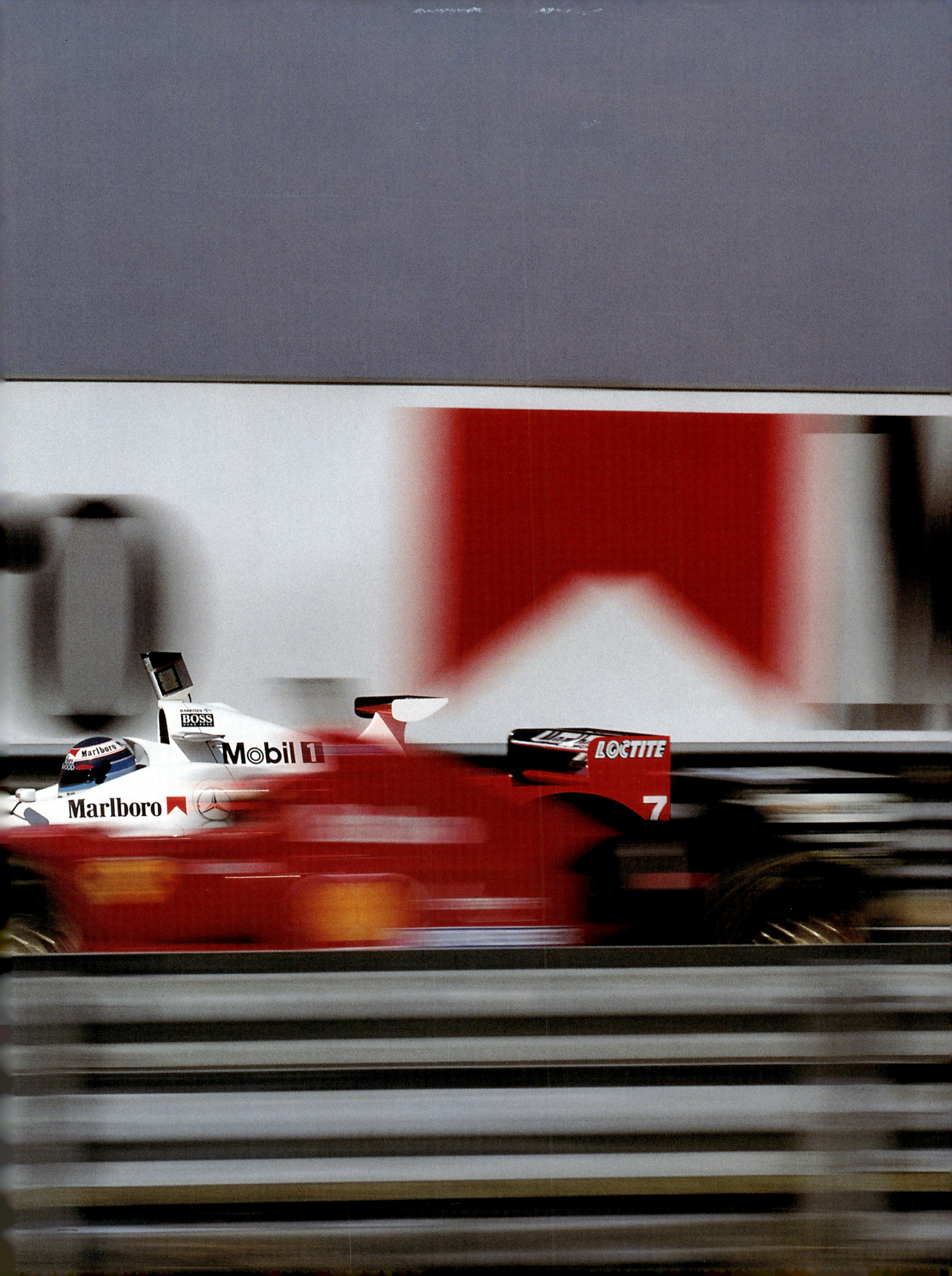
BOSS
Mobil 1
Marlboro
LOCTITE
7

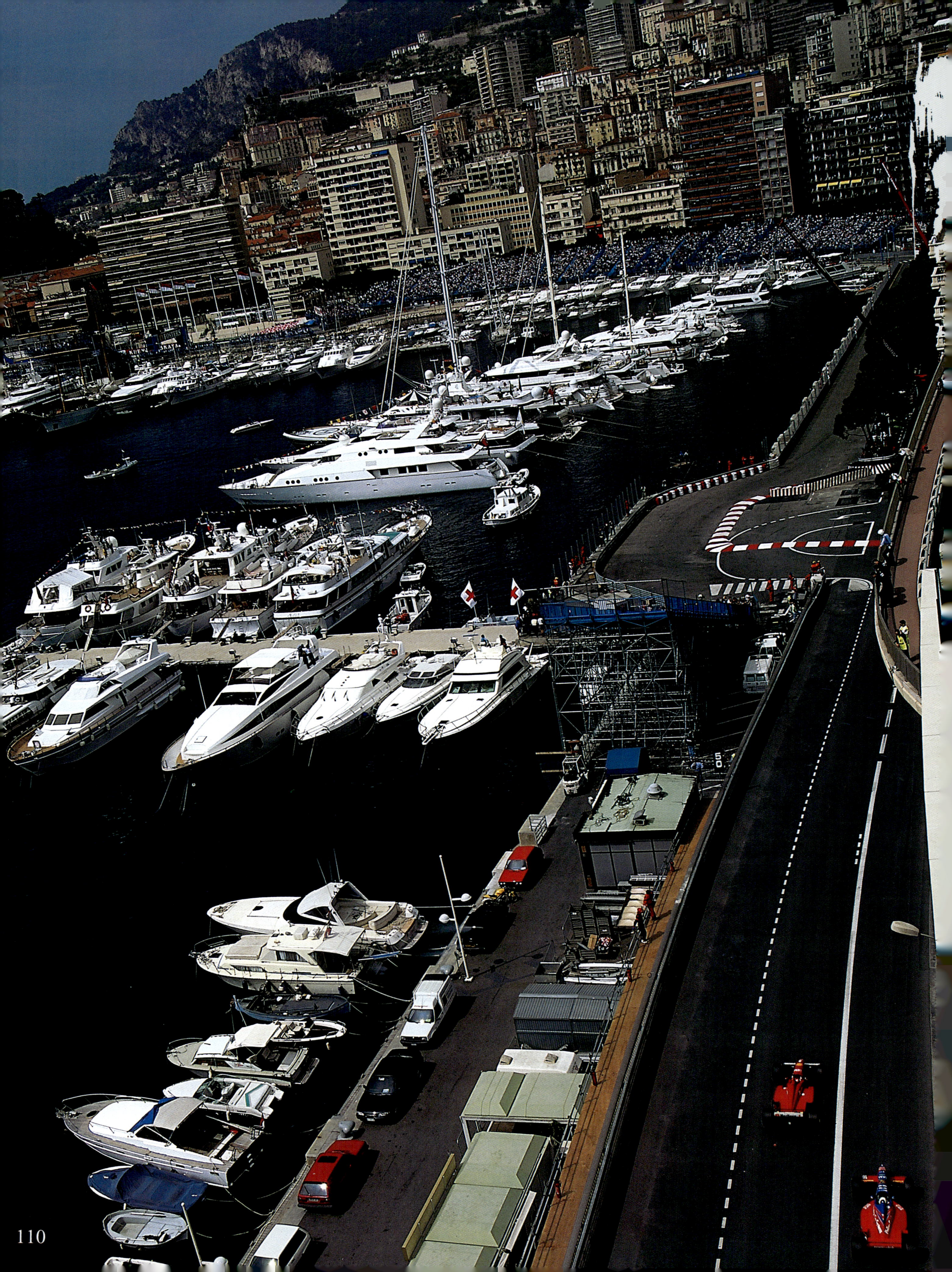

Als er 1996 in Monaco eine brillante Poleposition hinlegt, im Rennen aber sofort in die Leitschienen knallt, nimmt ihn Ferrari-Teamchef Jean Todt in Schutz: „Michael akzeptiert unsere Fehler, wir akzeptieren seine..."

In Monaco 1996, when he set a brilliant pole position, then immediately rammed into the planks at the start of the race, Ferrari team boss Jean Todt took him under his wing: "Michael accepts our mistakes, and we accept his... "

Nel 1996 a Montecarlo conquista brillantemente la pole position, ma in partenza finisce subito contro il guardrail. Jean Todt, direttore sportivo della Ferrari, prende le sue difese: "Michael accetta i nostri errori, e noi accettiamo i suoi..."

Ferrari 1996 war für Schumi ein Schwebezustand zwischen Mythos und <Sabotage>, wie Zeitungen, nach etlichen merkwürdigen Defekten mutmaßten. Der Motivationsschub, den er nach Maranello brachte, wurde durch seinen übernatürlichen Regensieg in Barcelona, errungen über Alesi und Villeneuve, nochmals verstärkt.

Driving for Ferrari in 1996 was like hovering in a state of suspense between myth and "sabotage" for Schumi - or so the newspapers conjectured after several strange defects. The motivation which he brought to Maranello became even stronger after his supernatural rain victory in Barcelona over Alesi and Villeneuve.

Nel 1996 la Ferrari per Schumi è una creatura che aleggia tra il mito e il 'sabotaggio', insinuano alcuni giornali dopo una serie di strani inconvenienti. Ma la ventata di motivazione che Schumi porta a Maranello viene ulteriormente rafforzata dalla "impossibile" vittoria conquistata nel diluvio di Barcellona davanti ad Alesi e Villeneuve.

113

Der Junge von nebenan wurde zum Superstar, und die Nation warf sich in seinen Windschatten. Schumacher platzt in eine Zeit rein, in der man ke

The boy from nextdoor became a superstar, and the nation followed in his slipstream. Schumacher came at a time when everyone was weary of n

Il ragazzo della porta accanto diventa una super-star e il Paese si mette nella sua scia. Schumacher "esplode" nel bel mezzo di un'epoca in cui non si v

astrophenmeldungen mehr hören mag und der Formel 1 die Idole ausgegangen sind. Und dem Volk die Träume von einer Insel der Seligen.

ut catastrophies, when Formula 1 had lost all its idols, and when the people had forgotten their dreams of Utopia.

sentire parlare di gravi incidenti, in cui la Formula 1 non ha piú miti da proporre e in cui la gente non coltiva piú il sogno dell'isola felice.

116

Ganz selten geht ihm die Straße aus, wie hier 1996 in Spa, aber das zeigt höchstens, daß sich hinter der vollendeten Fahrmaschine Schumacher doch ein Mensch aus Fleisch und Blut verbirgt. Dank seines athletischen Muskelkostüms werden solche Crashs verletzungsfrei absorbiert.

Rarely did he venture off the circuits, as he did here in Spa in 1996, but at least it showed that behind the perfect driving machine was a man of flesh and blood. Thanks to his athletic build such crashes passed without injury.

Solo raramente esce di pista, come nel 1996 a Spa, ma è la dimostrazione che dietro alla perfetta macchina da guida chiamata Schumacher c'è pur sempre un uomo in carne e ossa. Grazie alla sua costituzione atletica assorbe senza lesioni impatti come questo.

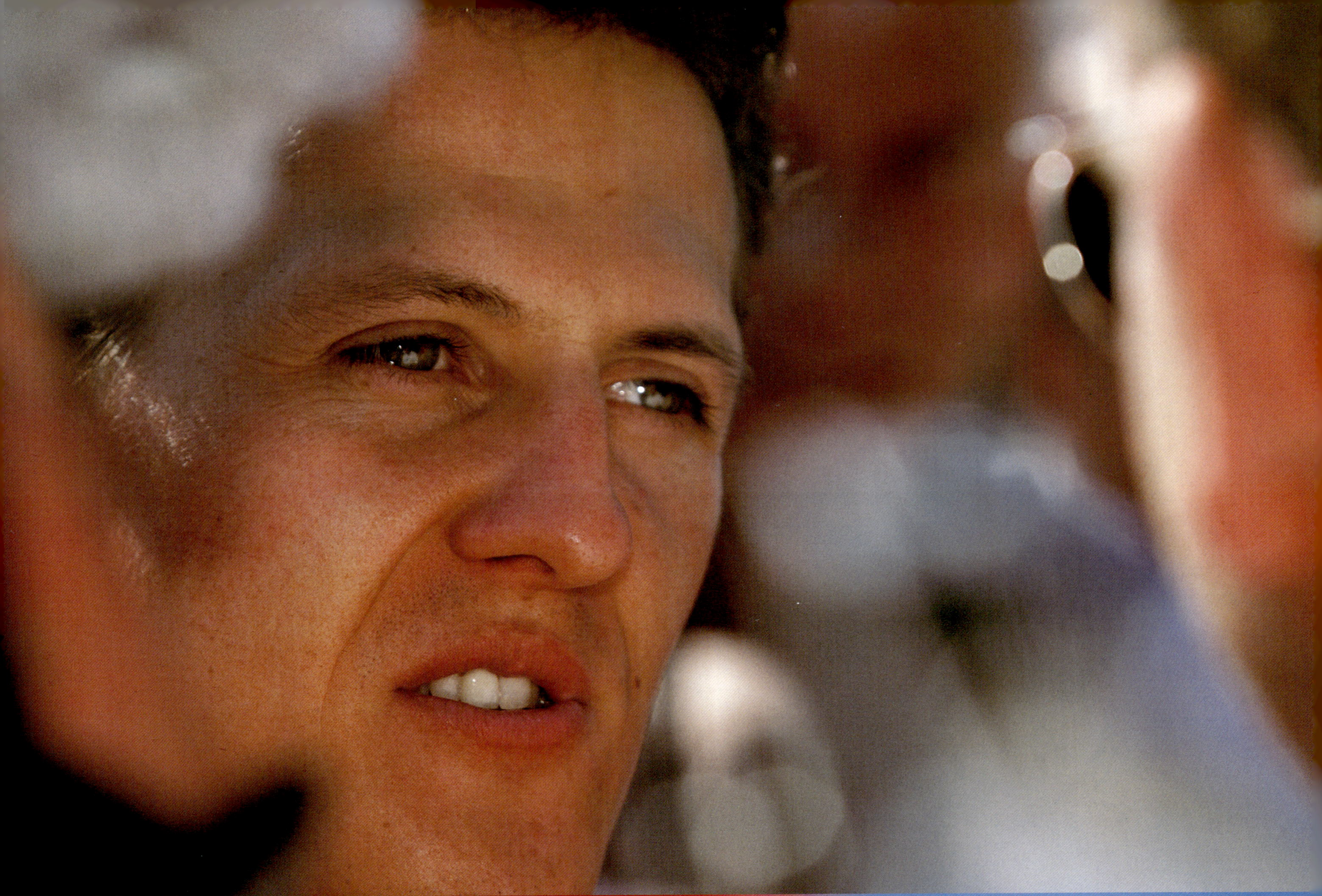

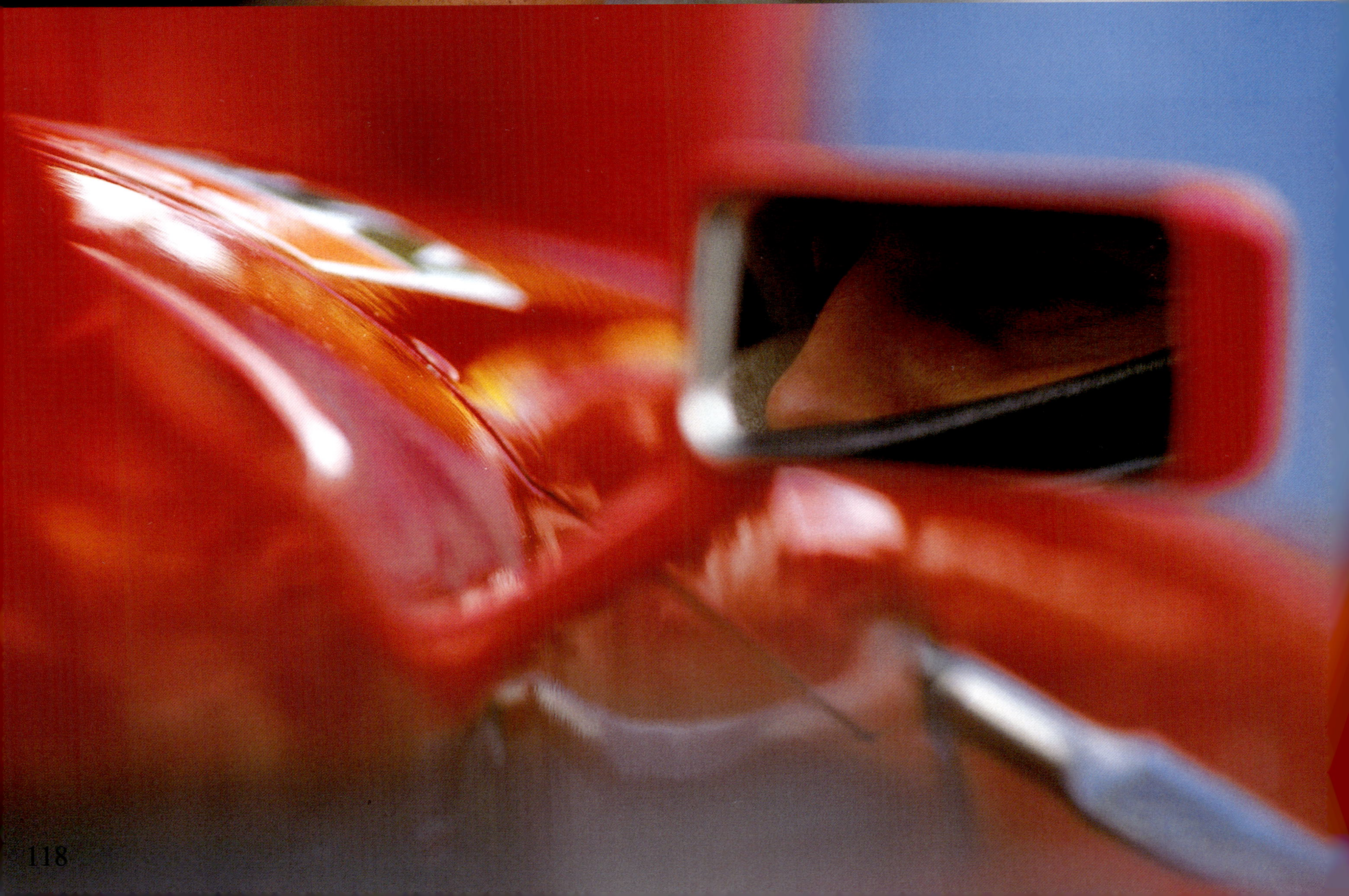

„Langsam fühle ich mich wie der König von Belgien", sagte Schumi nach seinem 21. Grand-Prix-Sieg, den er trotz defekter Lenkung am 25. August 1996 in Spa-Francorchamps gegen das Williams-Tandem Villeneuve Hill an Land zog.

"Gradually I begin to feel like the King of Belgium," said Schumi after his 21st Grand Prix win, which he landed, despite troublesome steering, on August 25th 1996 in Spa Francorchamps, against the Williams duo Villeneuve and Hill.

"A poco a poco mi sento come il re del Belgio", dice scherzando dopo la 21ma vittoria in un Gran Premio, conquistata, nonostante lo sterzo difettoso, il 25 agosto 1996 a Spa-Francorchamps contro il tandem Villeneuve-Hill della Williams.

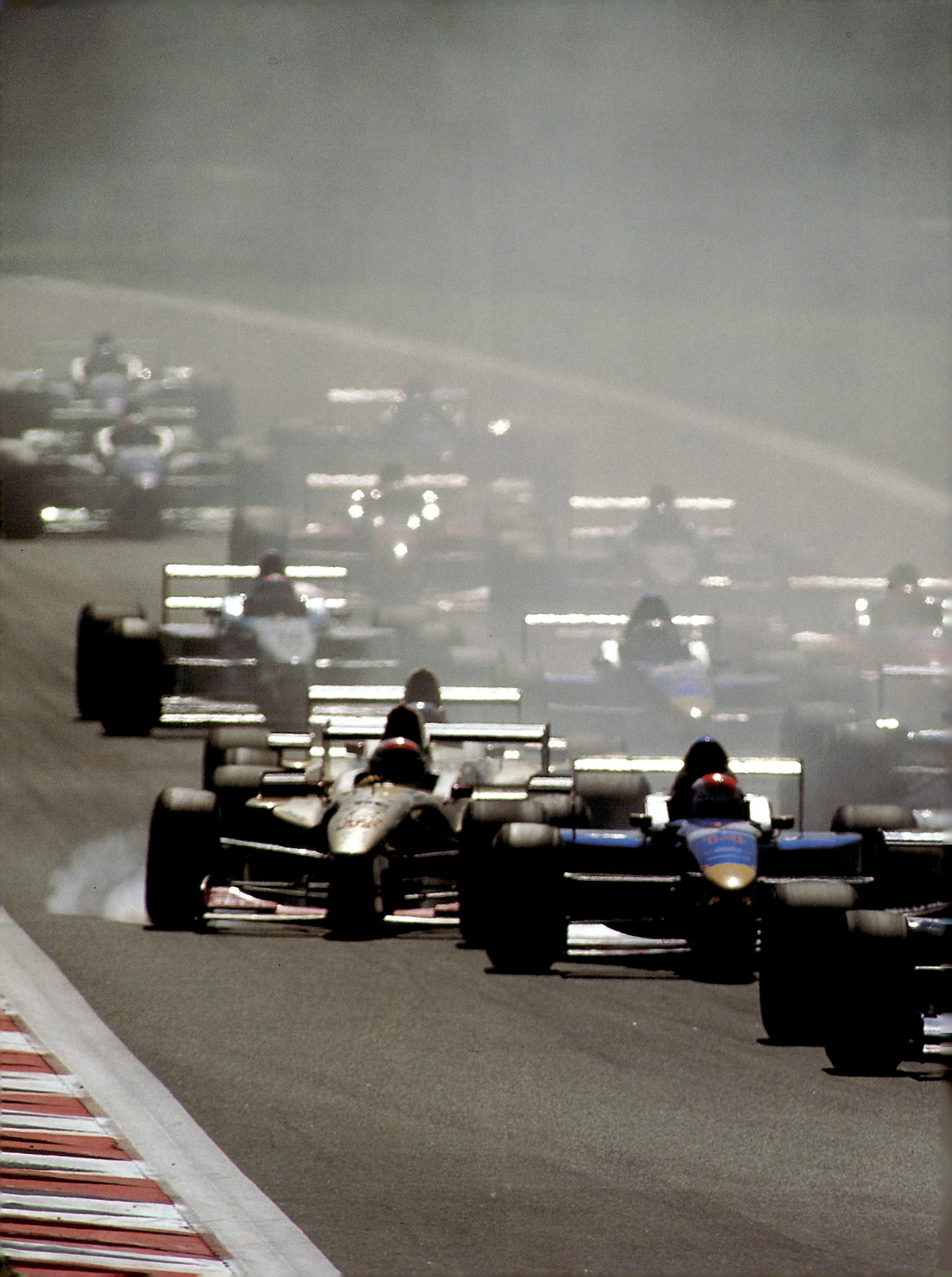

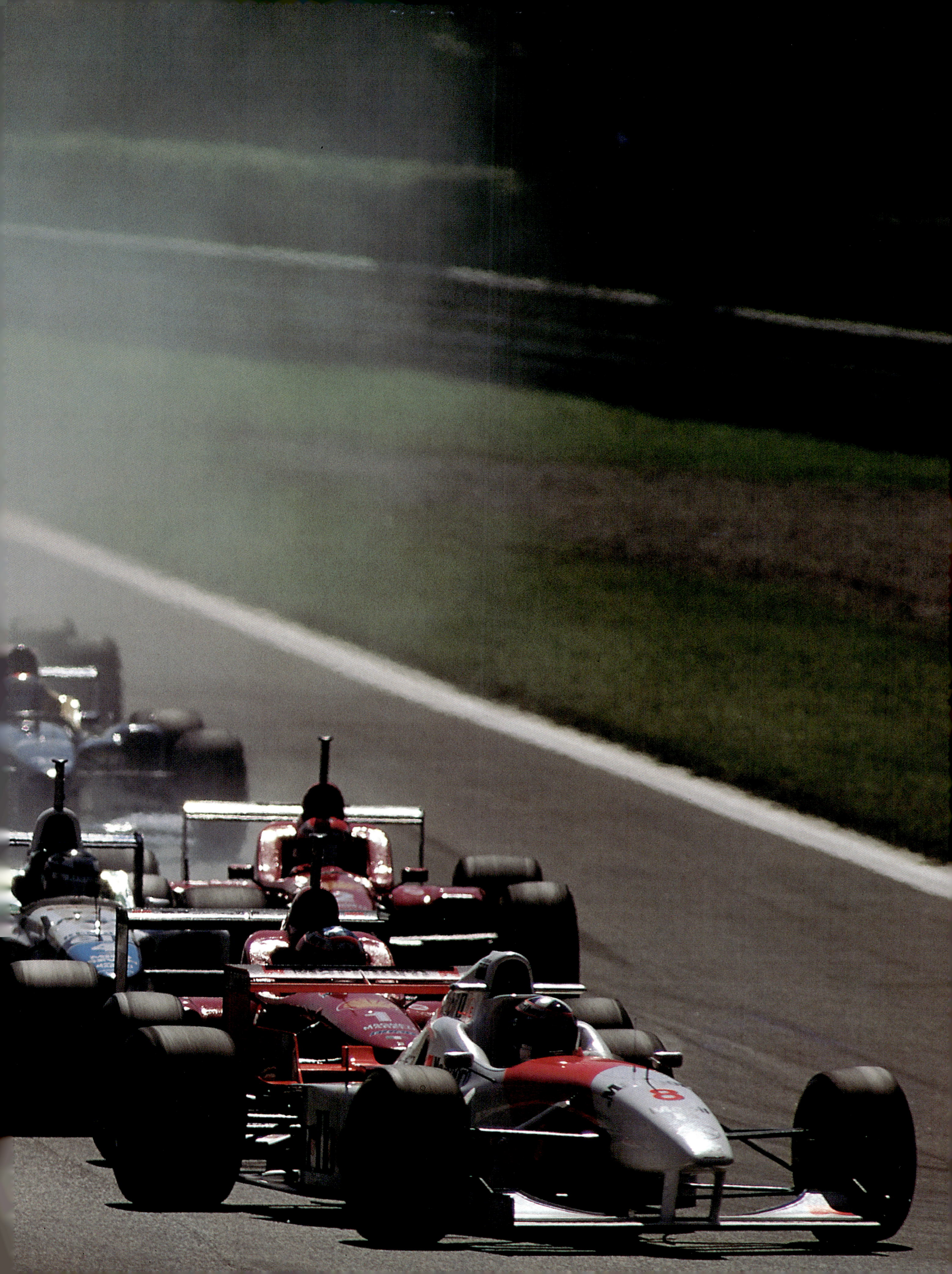

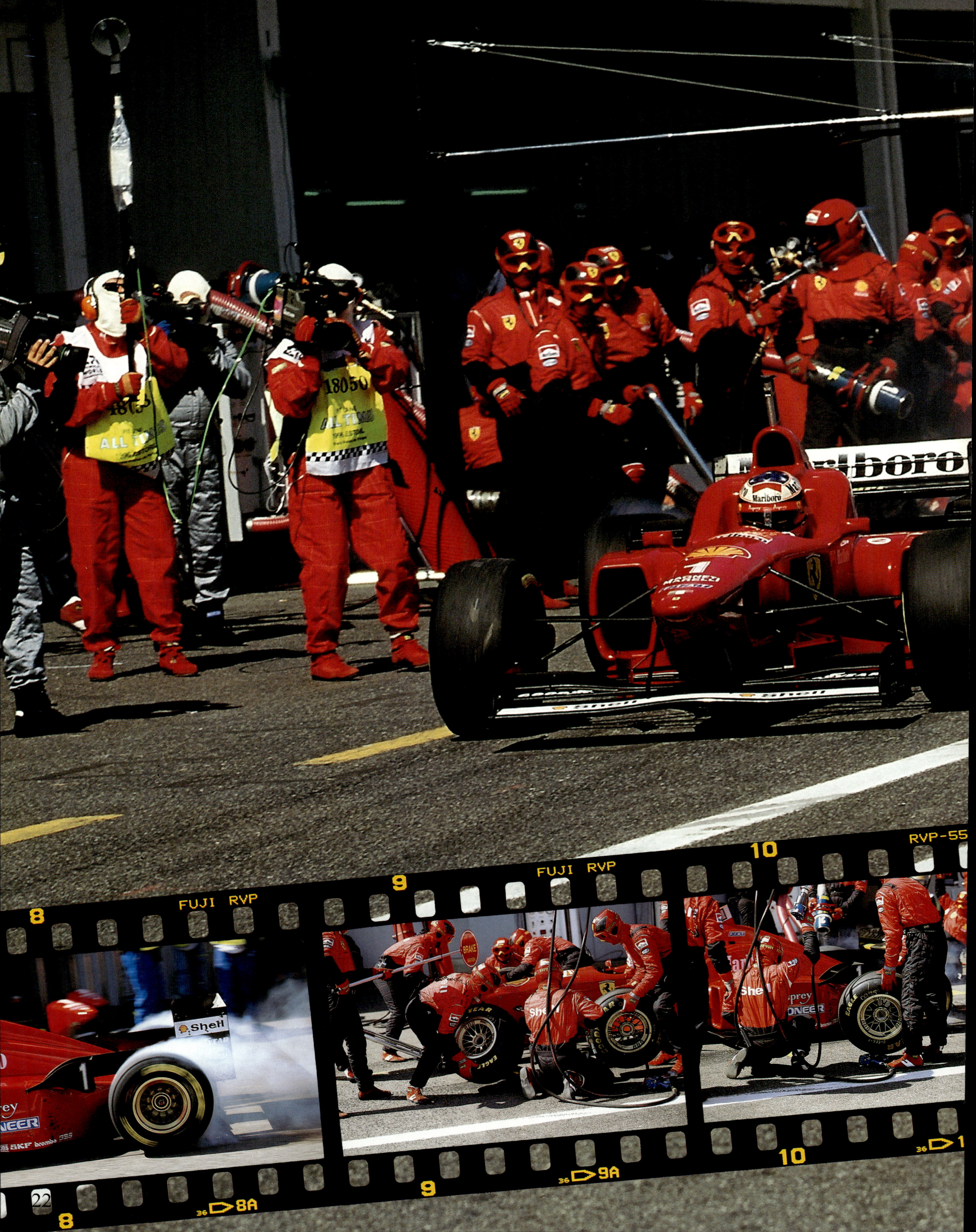
18050
FUJI RVP
RVP-55
Shell
Marlboro
BRAKE

Die Runden vor einem Boxenstopp, zu einem Boxenstopp und von einem Boxenstopp weg, fährt er jeweils optimal, immer an der Haftgrenze. Er trainiert diese Phase und nimmt den Gegnern wertvolle Sekunden ab.

He drives the laps before pitting, into the pits, and after the pitstop immaculately, and at the limit of what's possible. He specifically trains for this phase, and snatches precious seconds from his opponents.

I giri che precedono la sosta ai box, quelli della sosta vera e propria e quelli dopo la sosta stessa sono sempre perfetti, al limite dell'aderenza. Grazie alla particolare cura che dedica a questa fase della gara riesce a guadagnare secondi preziosi nei confronti degli avversari.

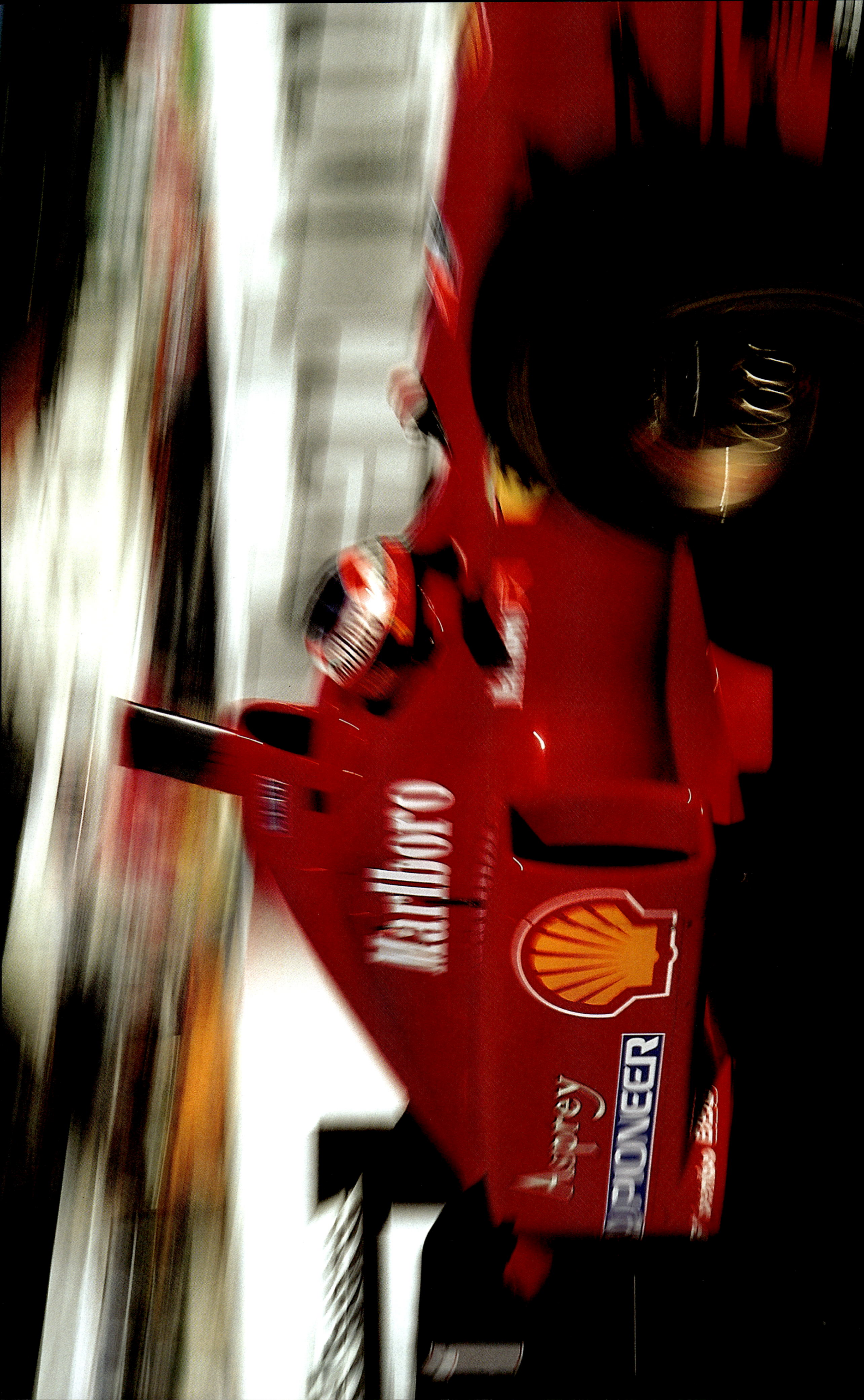
Marlboro
Asprey
PIONEER

Für Sicherheit im Straßenverkehr.

Europaweit!

Als Formel-1-Doppel-Weltmeister setzt Michael Schumacher auf eine optimale Fahrzeugsicherheit; beim Motorsport und im Straßenverkehr. Privat vertraut er auf die Kompetenz seines Partners DEKRA. DEKRA: Bei Haupt- und Abgasuntersuchungen, Fahrzeugbewertungen und Anbauabnahmen.

DEKRA

DEKRA e.V., Handwerkstr. 15, D-70565 Stuttgart, Tel.: (07 11) 78 61-0, Fax: (07 11) 78 61-22 40, Internet: http://www.dekra.de

Corinna Betsch wurde im August 1995 Frau Schumacher. Die Trauung erfolgte in der Kapelle des Hotels Petersberg in Bonn. An diesem Ambiente fanden die Großen dieser Welt immer schon Gefallen: Von Königin Elisabeth, Michail Gorbatschow, Bill Clinton, Kanzler Helmut Kohl bis zu den Schumachers...

In August 1995 Corinna Betsch became Mrs Schumacher. Vows were exchanged in the chapel at Petersberg castle near Bonn. The powerful and famous have all enjoyed the ambience of the castle: Queen Elizabeth, Michail Gorbachev, Bill Clinton, Chancellor Helmut Kohl...and the Schumachers...

Nell'agosto 1995 Corinna Betsch diventa la signora Schumacher. Le nozze vengono celebrate nella cappella del castello di Petersberg a Bonn, un ambiente che è sempre piaciuto ai grandi del mondo: dalla regina Elisabetta a Michail Gorbaciov, da Bill Clinton al cancelliere Kohl fino … ai coniugi Schumacher…

Eigentlich ist er ein Familienmensch, der Geborgenheit und Stabilität braucht, beides schenkt ihm Corinna. Am 20. Februar 1997 wurde ihre Tochter Gina Maria geboren. In Vufflens, zwischen Lausanne und Genf, in den Bergen nördlich des Genfer Sees, hat man ein neues Zuhause gefunden.

Actually, he's a family man needing security and stability. Corinna gives him both. On February 20th 1997 their daughter Gina Maria was born. In Vufflens, between Lausanne and Geneva in the mountains north of Lake Leman, they established a new home.

In realtà Schumi è un uomo che ama stare in famiglia, che ha bisogno di calore e sicurezza: due cose che Corinna sa dargli. Il 20 febbraio nasce la figlia Gina Maria. A Vufflens, sulle montagne a nord del Lago Lemano tra Losanna e Ginevra, trovano un nuovo domicilio.

Digitalanzeige Öldruck, Wassertemperatur, Tankinhalt
Digital display of oil pressure, water temperature, and fuel tank
Indicatore digitale pressione dell'olio, temperatura dell'acqua, contenuto serbatoio

Leerlauf
Neutral
In folle…

Anwählen der Digitalanzeige
Select digital display
Selezione dati digitali

Bremskraftverstellung vorne/hinten
Brake balance adjustment front/rear
Regolazione della frenata anteriore/posteriore

Ansprechverhalten Gaspedal
Throttle response
Risposta dell' acceleratore

Gemischanreicherung
Mixture enrichment
Arricchitore della miscela

Warnlampe
Warning lamp
Spia luminosa

Schaltwippe
Shift lever
Bilanciere del cambio

Rückwärtsgang
Reverse Gear
Retromarcia

Tempolimit
Speed limit
Limite di velocità

Sprechfunk
Radio system
Contatto radio

Elektronische
Bremskraftverstellung

Electronic brake
balance adjustment

Regolazione elettronica della frenata

Differentialsperre
Differential lock
Blocco del Differenziale

Kupplung
Clutch
Frizione

Anpassung Drehzahlbegrenzer
Setting of rev. limiter
Adattamento limitatore del regime

Kupplungsspiel
Clutch play
Il Gioco della frizione

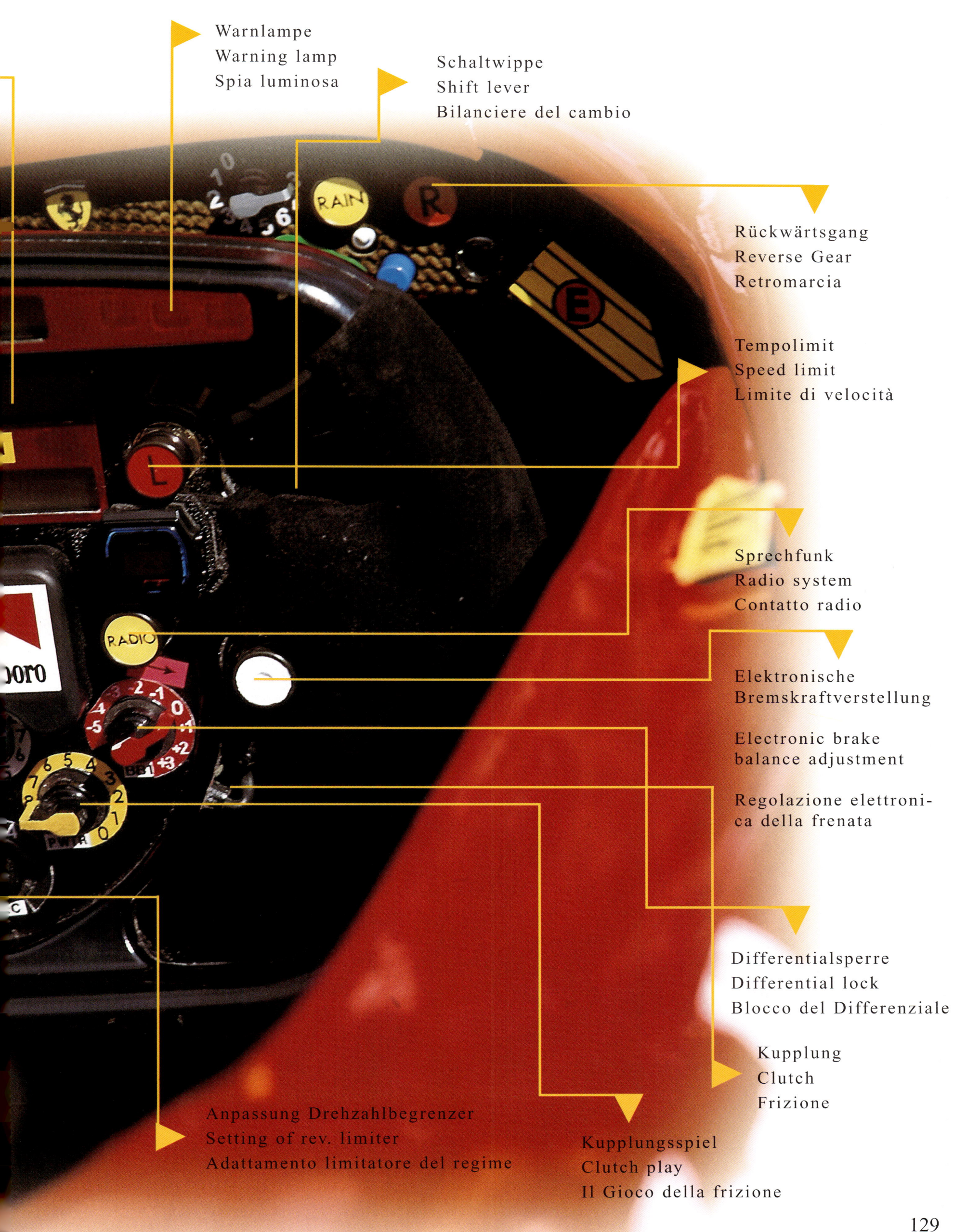

129

Shell und Ferrari - eine e

rfolgreiche Partnerschaft

▶ Shell und Ferrari - beide Unternehmen können auf eine lange und erfolgreiche Geschichte im Motorsport zurückblicken. Die Erfolgsbilanz ist unvergleichlich:

▶ Seit 1952 wurden gemeinsam sechs Fahrer- und zwei Konstrukteurs-Weltmeisterschaftstitel gewonnen - zu den 112 Grand-Prix-Siegen von Ferrari trug Shell 55 mal bei. Mit insgesamt 168 Grand-Prix-Siegen hat Shell in der Formel 1 mehr Titel als jede andere Mineralölgesellschaft eingefahren. Für Shell bedeutet dieses Engagement neben der Kooperation und Partnerschaft mit dem Team eine zielgerichtete globale Marketing-Maßnahme, um das Unternehmen und die Spitzenstellung seiner Produkte darzustellen und zu dokumentieren.

„Ferrari", sagte Präsident Luca die Montezemolo einst, „ist ein Monster, das regierbar gemacht werden muß." Erst im zweiten Jahr der Schumacher-Ära war der geschichtsträchtigste und wichtigste Rennstall der Formel 1 in seinen Schlüsselpositionen so durchgestylt, daß eine neue technische Saat aufkeimen konnte. „Michael", sagt Willy Weber, „ist der schnellste Konstrukteur der Welt, der baut ja mit." Ferrari, der Rennstall mit den größten Ressourcen, dem größten Anhang, den meisten Fans, dem aufregendsten Nimbus, ist stets auch in den Medien-Centern der Grand-Prix-Schauplätze (nächste Seite) das Thema Nummer eins.

"Ferrari," said President Luca di Montezemolo at one time, "is a monster which needs to be brought under control." It was only in the second year of the Schumacher era that the most legendary and important Formula 1 racing team was renovated in all its key positions, and ready for the new technical seed to germinate.
"Michael", says Willy Weber, "is the fastest designer in the world, it's always on his mind…"
Ferrari, the stable with the greatest resources, the largest support, the most fans, the most exciting aura, is always topic number one in the media centres at the Grands Prix, as well.

"La Ferrari", dice una volta il suo presidente Luca di Montezemolo, "è un mostro che vuol essere dominato". Solo nell'anno secondo dell'èra Schumacher la scuderia più prestigiosa e più importante della Formula 1 è ristrutturata nelle posizioni-chiave in modo da consentire una nuova fioritura tecnica.
"Michael", dice Willy Weber, "è il progettista più veloce del mondo, perchè collabora in prima persona al progetto."
La Ferrari, la scuderia dalle maggiori risorse, dalla tifoseria più nutrita, dal seguito più entusiasta, dal mito più emozionante di tutta la Formula 1, costituisce sempre l'argomento del giorno anche nei "media center" sui campi di gara (pagina seguente).

Marlboro
Shell

Marlboro
Shell
GOODYEAR
EAGLE
BBS

Marlboro
Shell

Marlboro
Shell

Marlboro

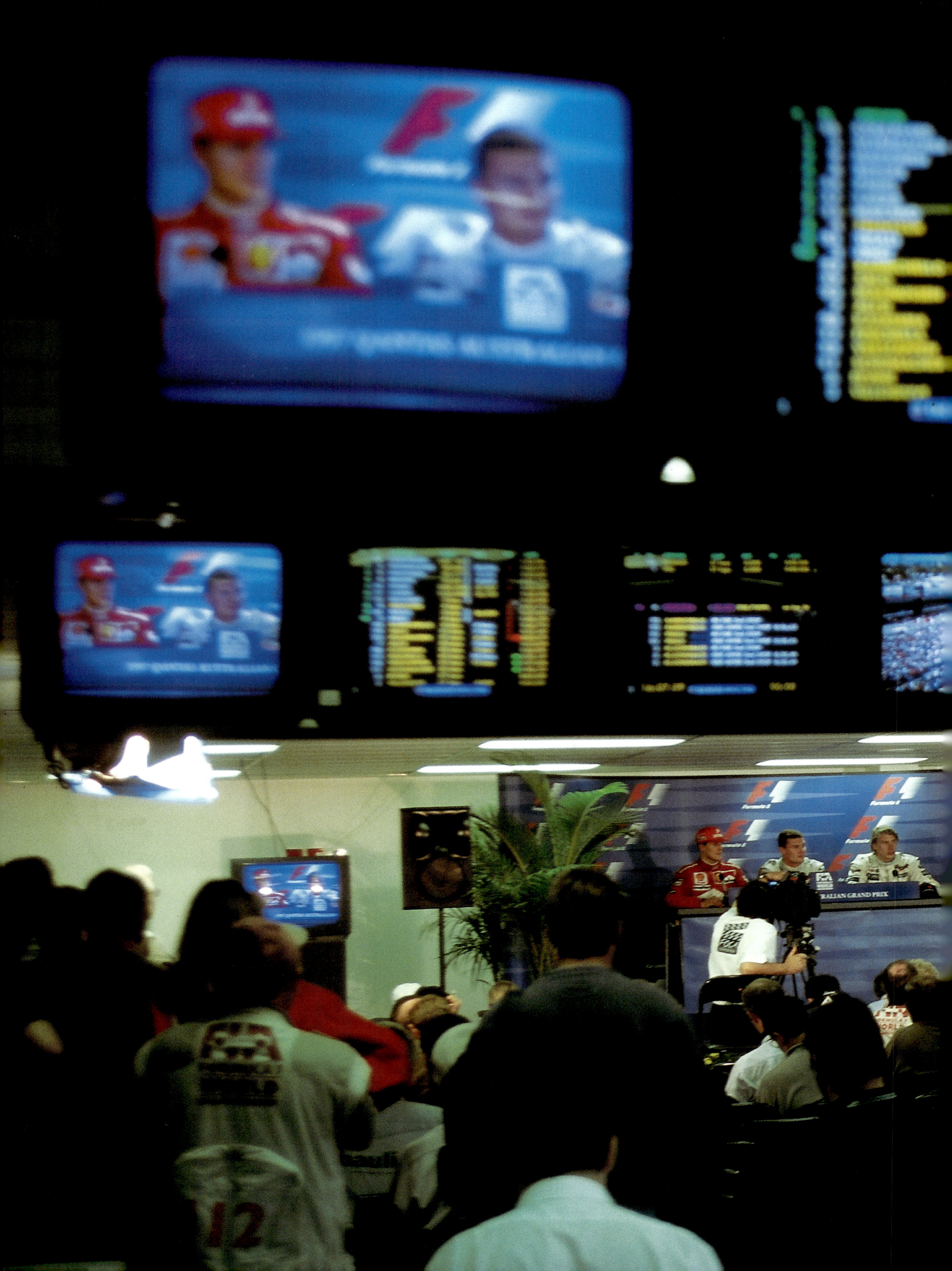

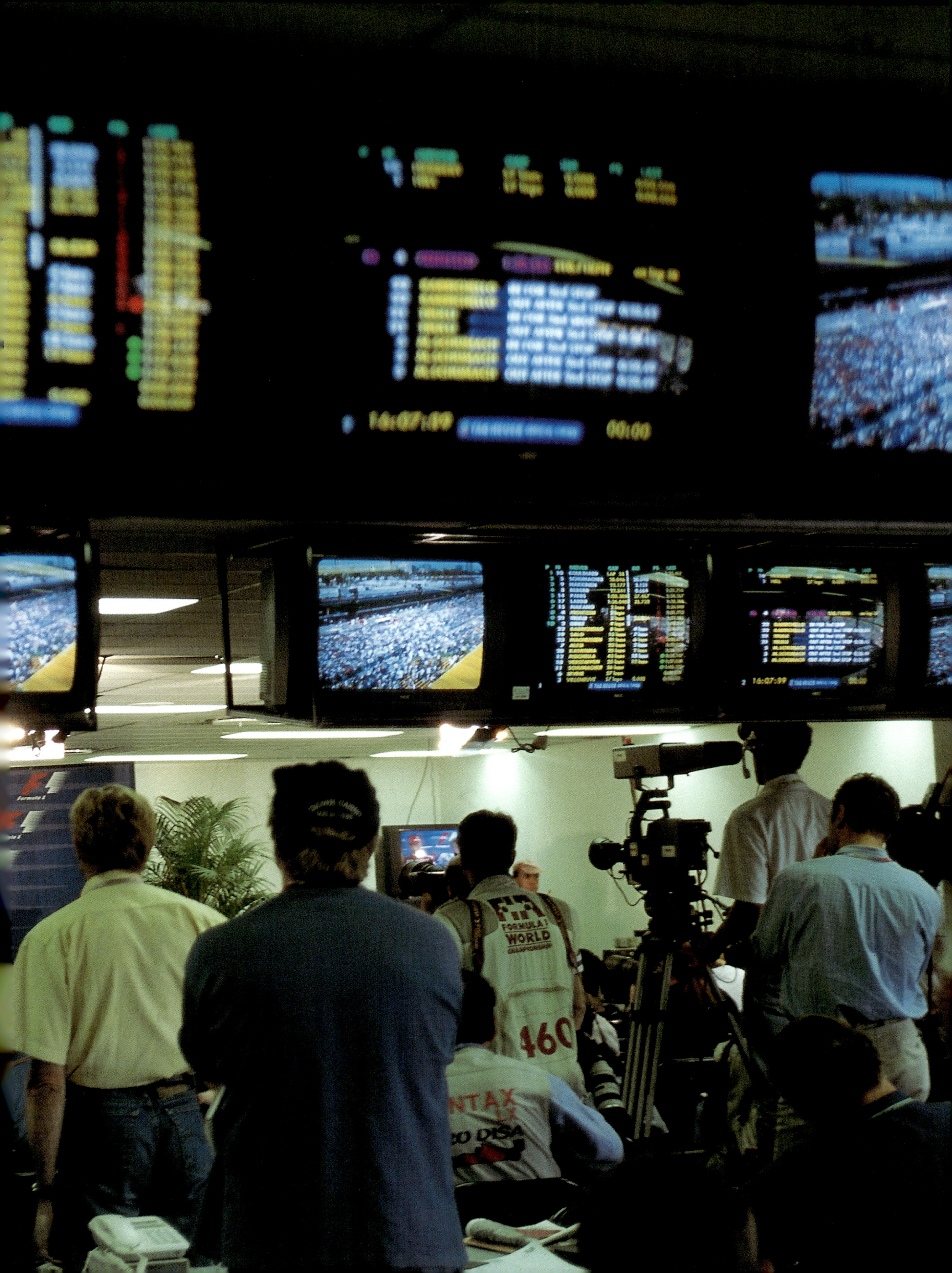
16:07:39
00:00
FORMULA 1
WORLD
CHAMPIONSHIP
460

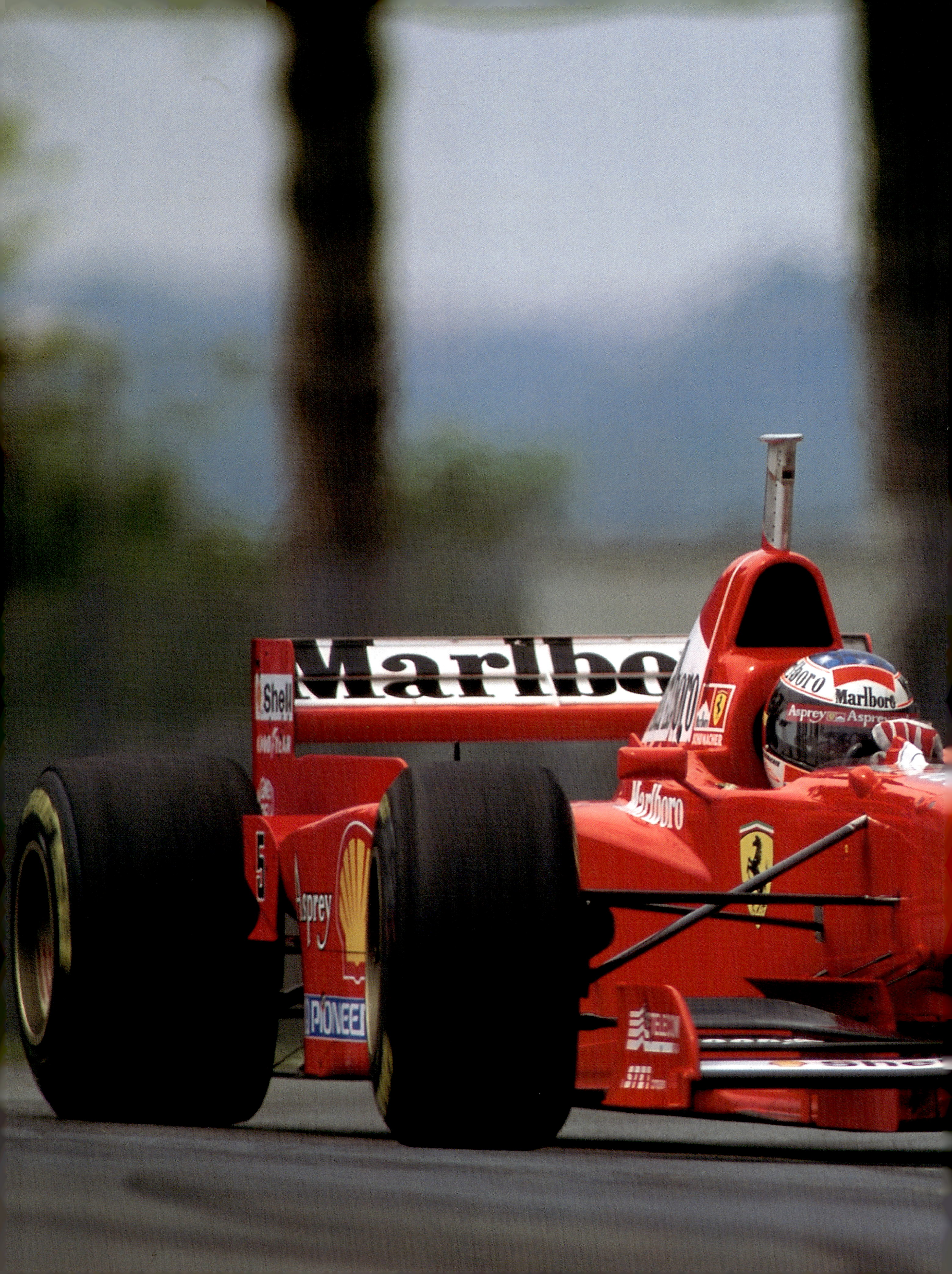
Shell
Marlboro
Marlboro
Asprey
PIONEER

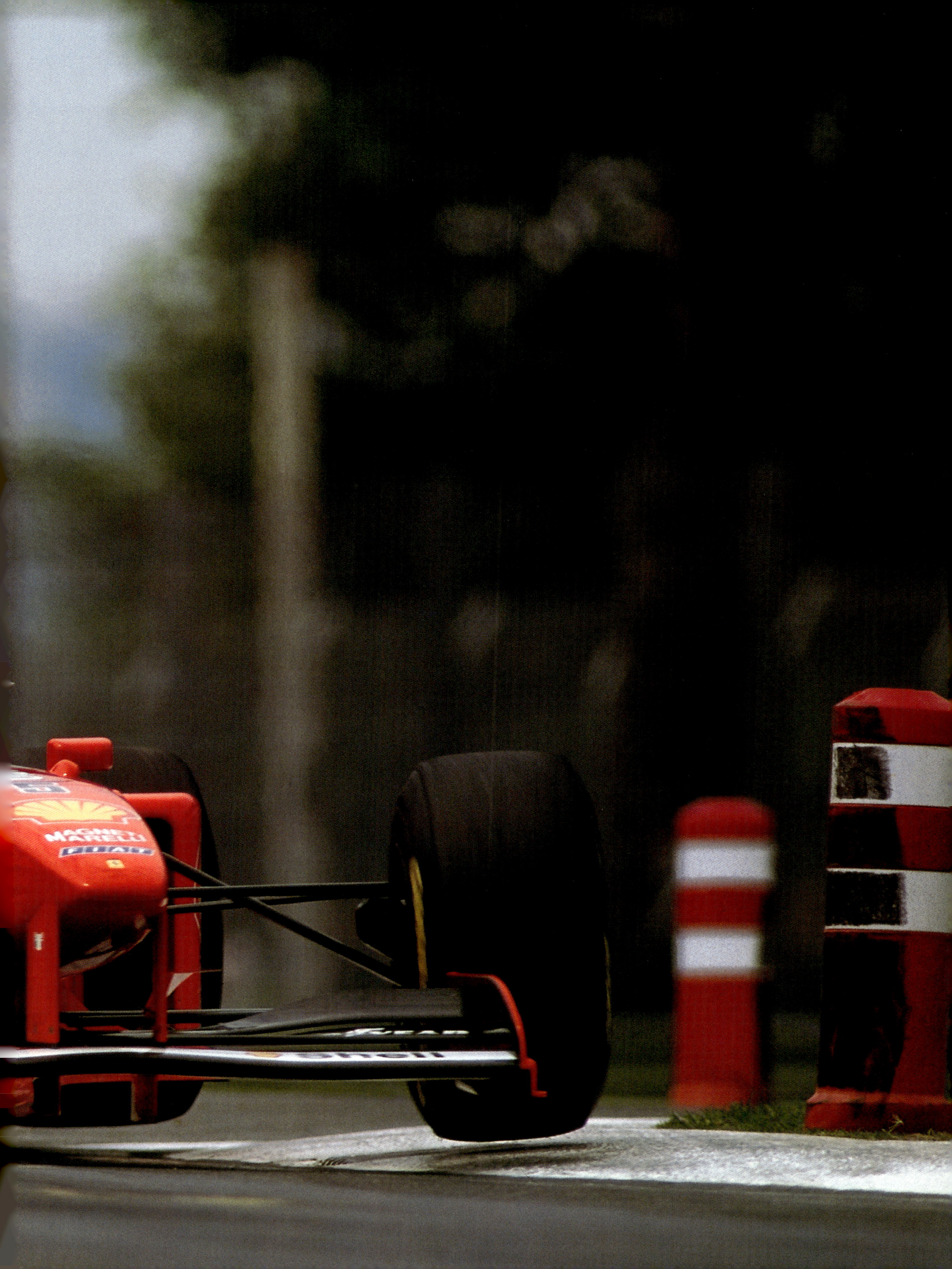
MAGNETI MARELLI
FIAT

Michael Schumacher's Qualifyin

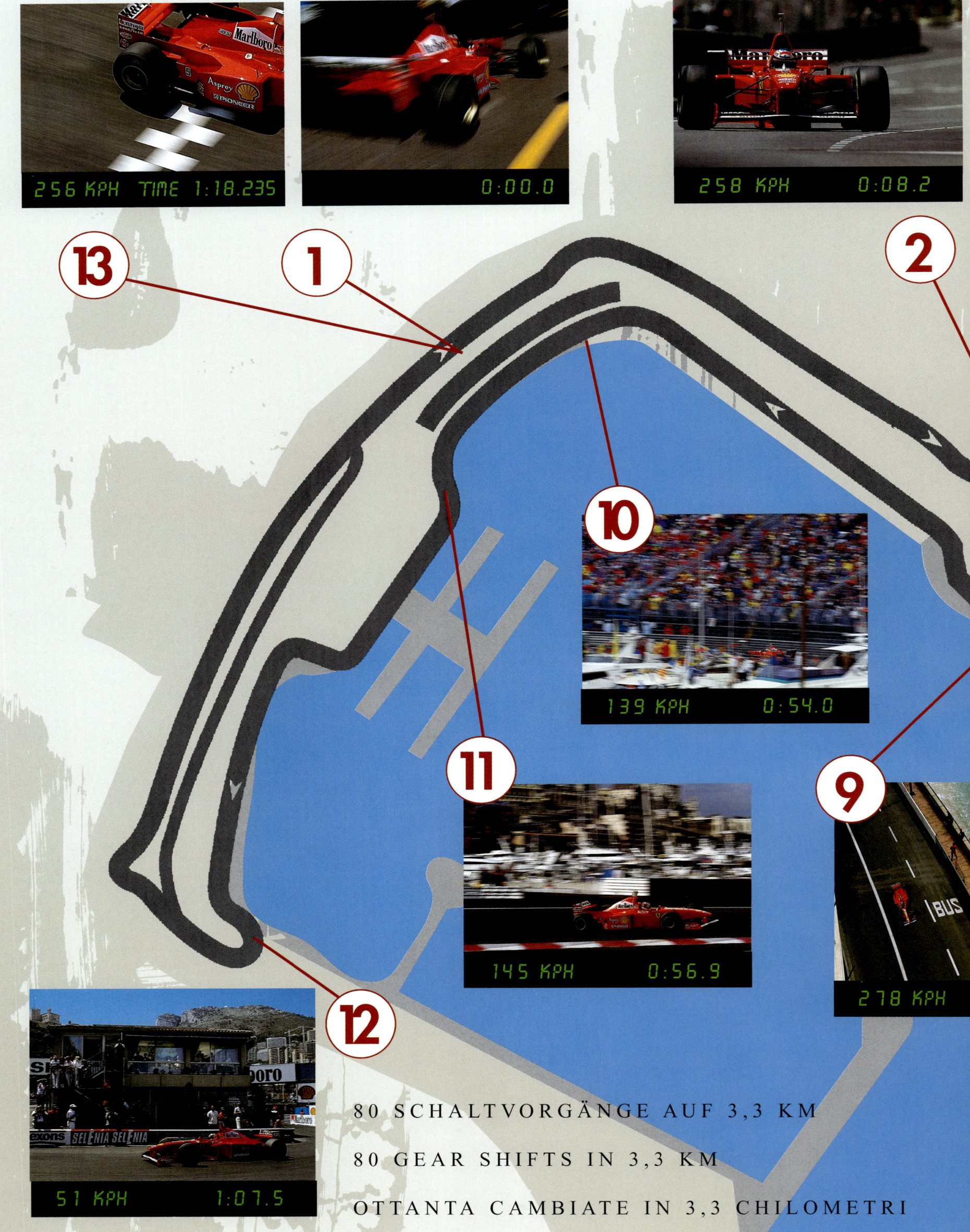

256 KPH   TIME 1:18.235

0:00.0

258 KPH   0:08.2

139 KPH   0:54.0

145 KPH   0:56.9

278 KPH

51 KPH   1:07.5

80 SCHALTVORGÄNGE AUF 3,3 KM

80 GEAR SHIFTS IN 3,3 KM

OTTANTA CAMBIATE IN 3,3 CHILOMETRI

-Runde Grand Prix Monaco 1997

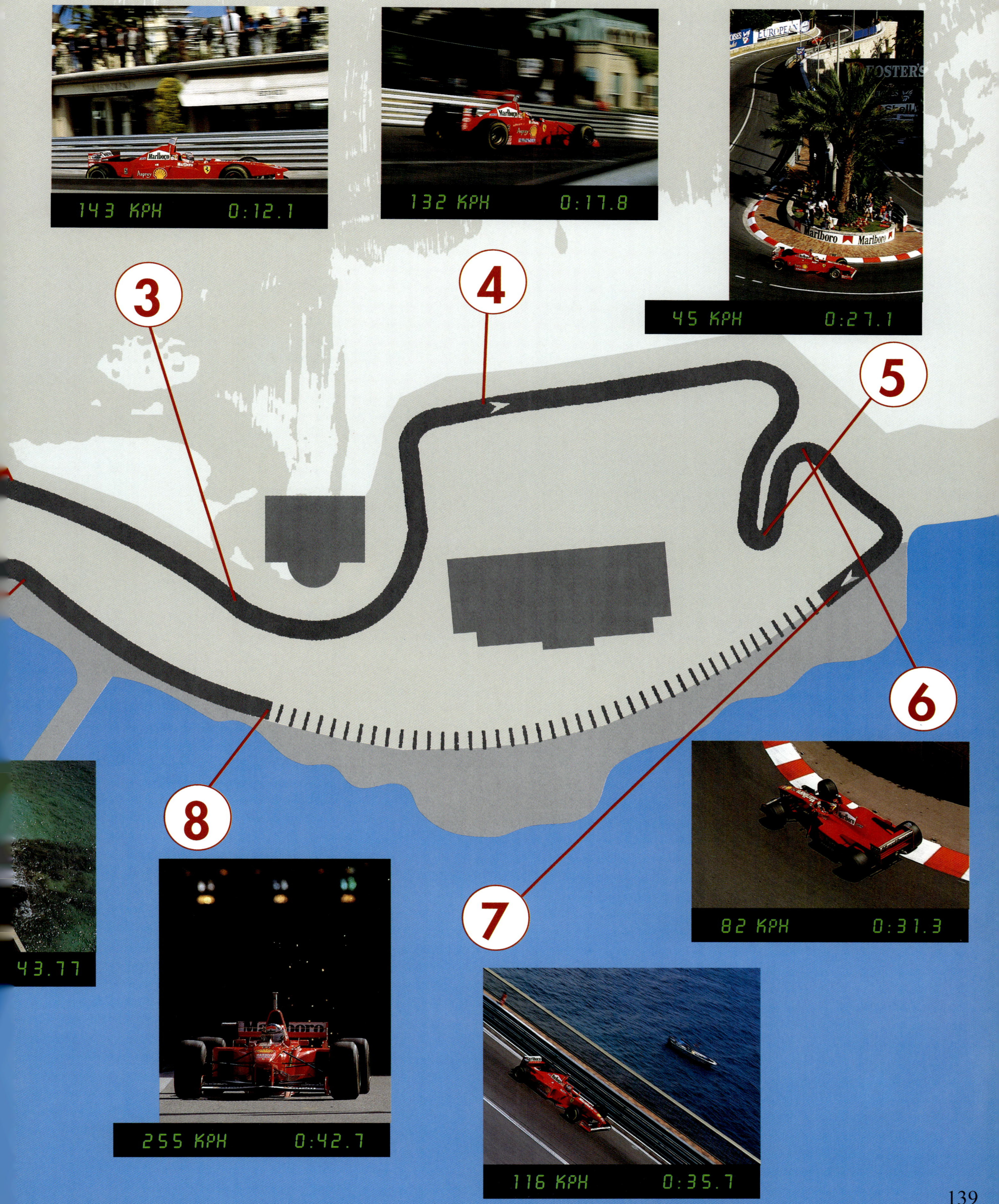

143 KPH 0:12.1

132 KPH 0:17.8

45 KPH 0:27.1

3

4

5

6

7

8

43.77

255 KPH 0:42.7

82 KPH 0:31.3

116 KPH 0:35.7

139

Im Monaco Grand Prix 1997 bewies er, daß der Schumacher-Faktor mit 25 Millionen Dollar pro Jahr nicht überbezahlt ist: Schumi ging gewissermaßen übers Wasser - bis zur endgültigen Dusche - mit Champagner.

In the 1997 Monaco Grand Prix, he proved that the Schumacher-factor is not overpaid with $US25 million per year. Schumi practically walked on water and was rewarded with a champagne shower.

Il Gran Premio di Montecarlo del 1997 dimostra che il prezzo del fattore Schumacherì - 25 milioni di dollari all'anno - non è esagerato: "camminando sull'acqua" Schumi si avvia alla doccia finale di champagne.

Marlboro
Marlboro
Marlboro
Asprey
PIONEER

Marlboro
Asprey
PIONEER

Marlboro

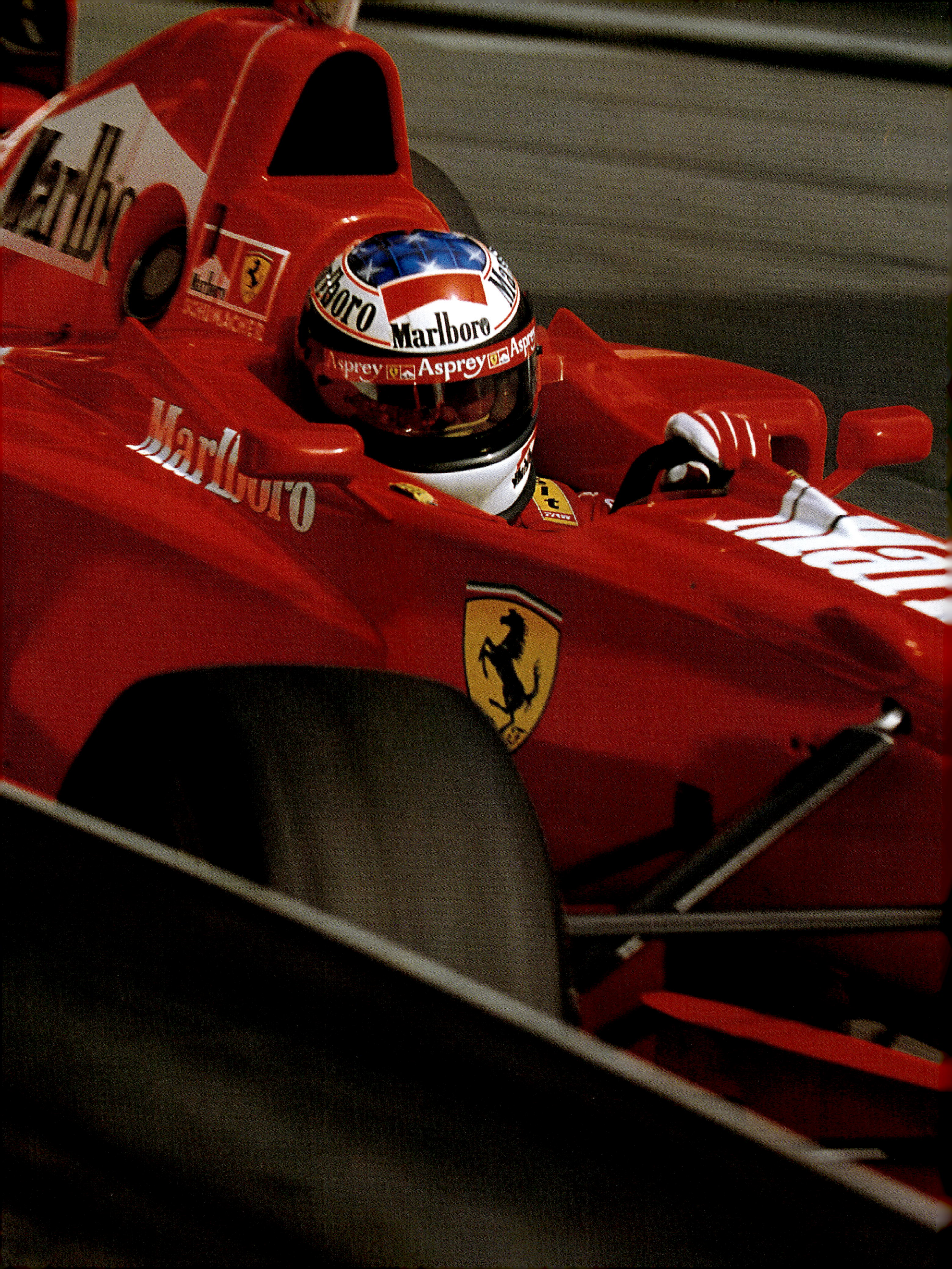
Marlboro
Asprey
Asprey
Marlboro

GOOD to be №1.

Mit einem weiteren Sieg in Barcelona macht Goodyear zum 350. Mal das Rennen in der Formel 1. Wer die härteste Teststrecke der Welt so erfolgreich meistert, sorgt dafür, daß auch Sie bei den schwersten Anforderungen des täglichen Lebens gut ankommen.

FORMEL 1 — 350. SIEG

Good to know.

GOOD/**YEAR**

s   t   a   t

1984 Deutscher Kart-Juniorenmeister

1985 Deutscher Kart-Juniorenmeister   Kart-Junioren-Vizeweltmeister

1986 Deutsche Kartmeisterschaft   Platz 3 / Fahrzeug Kali

1987 Platz 1 / Fahrzeug Kali / Parilla

1988

Formel König Platz 1

Formel Ford Platz 6 / Fahrzeug Van Diemen

Platz 2 Europameisterschaft

1989 Deutsche Formel-3-Meisterschaft

Platz 2   Reynard 893

1990

Platz 1   Reynard F 390

Platz 5 / Mercedes   Gruppe C Sportwagen

1991 Gruppe C Sportwagen-Weltmeisterschaft

Platz 9 / Mercedes

Formel 1   Platz 12   Jordan/ Benetton

s t i k

michael schumacher

1992
Formel I - Weltmeisterschaft

1992	Platz 3	Benetton-Ford
1993	Platz 4	Benetton-Ford
1994	Platz 1	Benetton-Ford
1995	Platz 1	Benetton-Renault
1996	Platz 3	Ferrari

WORLD CHAMPION CONSTRUCTORS

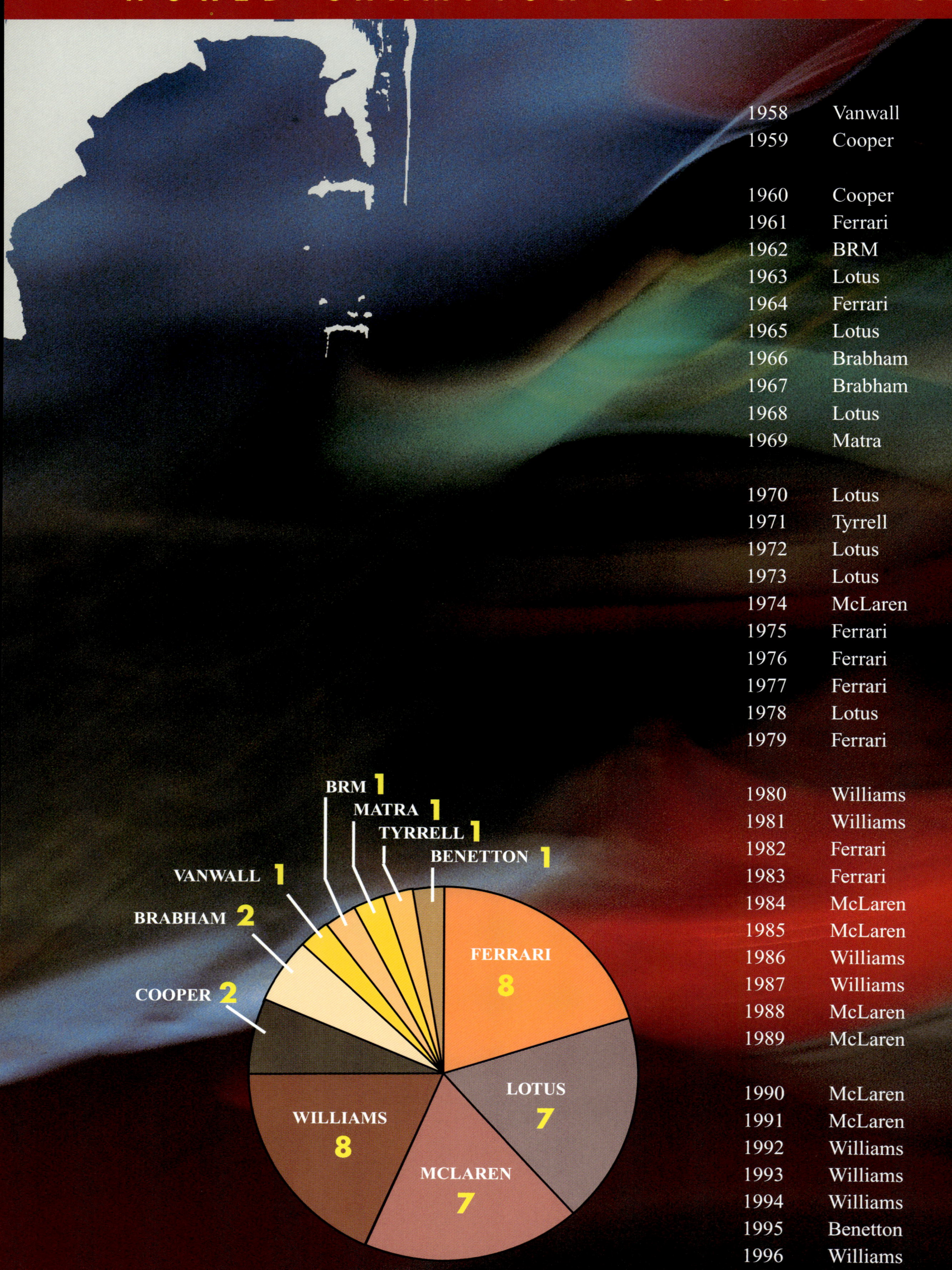

1958	Vanwall
1959	Cooper
1960	Cooper
1961	Ferrari
1962	BRM
1963	Lotus
1964	Ferrari
1965	Lotus
1966	Brabham
1967	Brabham
1968	Lotus
1969	Matra
1970	Lotus
1971	Tyrrell
1972	Lotus
1973	Lotus
1974	McLaren
1975	Ferrari
1976	Ferrari
1977	Ferrari
1978	Lotus
1979	Ferrari
1980	Williams
1981	Williams
1982	Ferrari
1983	Ferrari
1984	McLaren
1985	McLaren
1986	Williams
1987	Williams
1988	McLaren
1989	McLaren
1990	McLaren
1991	McLaren
1992	Williams
1993	Williams
1994	Williams
1995	Benetton
1996	Williams

BRM 1
MATRA 1
TYRRELL 1
BENETTON 1
VANWALL 1
BRABHAM 2
COOPER 2
FERRARI 8
LOTUS 7
WILLIAMS 8
MCLAREN 7

WORLD CHAMPION DRIVERS

Year	Driver	Car	Tyres
1950	Farina (I)	Alfa Romeo	Pirelli
1951	Fangio (RA)	Alfa Romeo	Pirelli
1952	Ascari (I)	Ferrari	Pirelli
1953	Ascari (I)	Ferrari	Pirelli
1954	Fangio (RA)	Mercedes / Maserati	Pirelli / Conti
1955	Fangio (RA)	Mercedes	Continental
1956	Fangio (RA)	Lancia / Ferrari	Englebert
1957	Fangio (RA)	Maserati	Pirelli
1958	Hawthorn (GB)	Ferrari	Englebert
1959	Brabham (Aus)	Cooper-Climax	Dunlop
1960	Brabham (Aus)	Cooper-Climax	Dunlop
1961	P Hill (USA)	Ferrari	Dunlop
1962	G Hill (GB)	BRM	Dunlop
1963	Clark (GB)	Lotus-Climax	Dunlop
1964	Surtees (GB)	Ferrari	Dunlop
1965	Clark (GB)	Lotus-Climax	Dunlop
1966	Brabham (Aus)	Brabham-Repco	Goodyear
1967	Hulme (NZ)	Brabham-Repco	Goodyear
1968	G Hill (GB)	Lotus Ford	Firestone
1969	Stewart (GB)	Matra Ford	Dunlop
1970	Rindt (Aut)	Lotus Ford	Firestone
1971	Stewart (GB)	Tyrrell Ford	Goodyear
1972	Fittipaldi (Brz)	Lotus Ford	Firestone
1973	Lauda (Aut)	Tyrrell Ford	Goodyear
1974	Hunt (GB)	McLaren Ford	Goodyear
1975	Lauda (Aut)	Ferrari	Goodyear
1976	Hunt (GB)	McLaren Ford	Goodyear
1977	Lauda (Aut)	Ferrari	Goodyear
1978	Andretti (USA)	Lotus Ford	Goodyear
1979	Scheckter (SA)	Ferrari	Michelin
1980	Jones (Aus)	Williams Ford	Goodyear
1981	Piquet (Brz)	Brabham Ford	Goodyear / Michelin
1982	Rosberg (SF)	Williams Ford	Goodyear
1983	Piquet (Brz)	Brabham BMW	Michelin
1984	Lauda (Aut)	McLaren TAG Porsche	Michelin
1985	Prost (F)	McLaren TAG Porsche	Goodyear
1986	Prost (F)	McLaren TAG Porsche	Goodyear
1987	Piquet (Brz)	Williams Honda	Goodyear
1988	Senna (Brz)	McLaren Honda	Goodyear
1989	Prost (F)	McLaren Honda	Goodyear
1990	Senna (Brz)	McLaren Honda	Goodyear
1991	Senna (Brz)	McLaren Honda	Goodyear
1992	Mansell (GB)	Williams Renault	Goodyear
1993	Prost (F)	Williams Renault	Goodyear
1994	Schumacher (D)	Benetton Ford	Goodyear
1995	Schumacher (D)	Benetton Renault	Goodyear
1996	Hill (GB)	Williams Renault	Goodyear

Michael denkt, Willy lenkt: Schumacher und Weber wurden zum Synonym für wunderbare Geldvermehrung. „Michael und Ralf wissen, daß ich einzig und allein Erfolge verkaufen kann", sagt der Manager mit Hinblick auf den zweiten Schumacher. Die Strategie ist vorprogrammiert, Ralfs Höhenflug nicht mehr aufzuhalten.

Michael und Ralf sind so unterschiedliches Obst wie Apfel und Banane. Michael ist introvertiert, Ralf extrovertiert. Michael ist pflegeleichter, Ralf abgebrühter, trickreicher. Ralf hinterfragt alles und fordert eine logische Erklärung. Michael ist experimentierfreudiger, er sucht ständig nach neuen Lösungen. So oder so: Sie sind das schnellste Brüderpaar der Welt.

Nächste Seite...

Michael rides, Willy guides: Schumacher and Weber became a synonym for the miraculous multiplying of money, "Michael and Ralf realise that there's only one thing I can really sell - and that's success," said the manager with a meaningful glance at the second Schumacher. The strategy is mapped out and Ralf's rocket upwards can't be reined in.

Michael and Ralf are as different as chalk and cheese. Michael is introverted, Ralf extroverted. Michael is easy to handle, Ralf tougher and more wily. Ralf questions everything and wants a logical explanation. Michael is a fan of experimentation, constantly on the lookout for new solutions. Either way, they are the fastest brothers on earth.

Next page...

Michael propone, Willy dispone: il binomio Schumacher/Weber diventa sinonimo di una stupefacente moltiplicazione dei soldi: "Michael e Ralf sanno che io posso vendere unicamente il successo", dice il manager con un occhio rivolto a "Schumacher secondo". La strategia è prestabilita, la carriera di Ralf è folgorante e inarrestabile.

Piú diversi non potrebbero essere: Michael e Ralf. Michael è introverso, Ralf estroverso. Michael è piú affabile, Ralf piú duro e astuto. Ralf vuol sapere tutto nel dettaglio e pretende una spiegazione logica. Michael ama l'esperimento, la ricerca incessante di nuove soluzioni. In ogni caso sono i fratelli piú veloci del mondo...

Alla prossima puntata.

149

150

Fortsetzung folgt.
To be continued.
segue.